LAKE
AND
POND

APRIL PULLEY SAYRE

TWENTY-FIRST CENTURY BOOKS

A Division of Henry Holt and Company
• New York •

to my many excellent teachers, including
Lasher, Mrs. Paouris, and Mrs. Joye.

ACKNOWLEDGMENTS

ohn Waldman of the Hudson River Foundation
berti of Notre Dame University for reviewing
t.

Twenty-First Century Books
A Division of Henry Holt and Company, Inc.
115 West 18th Street
New York, NY 10011

Henry Holt® and colophon are trademarks of
Henry Holt and Company, Inc.
Publishers since 1866

Library of Congress Cataloging-in-Publication Data
Sayre, April Pulley.
Lake and pond / April Pulley Sayre.—1st ed.
p. cm.—(Exploring earth's biomes)
Includes index.
Summary: Discusses the lake and pond biomes and how each
is affected by the environment and people.
1. Lake ecology—Juvenile literature. 2. Pond ecology—Juvenile literature.
3. Lakes—Juvenile literature. 4. Ponds—Juvenile literature. 5. Lake ecology—
North America—Juvenile literature. 6. Pond ecology—North America—Juvenile
literature. 7. Lakes—North America—Juvenile literature. 8. Ponds—North
America—Juvenile literature. [1. Lakes. 2. Ponds. 3. Lake ecology. 4. Pond ecology.
5. Ecology.] I. Title. II. Series: Sayre, April Pulley. Exploring earth's biomes.
QH541.5.L3S33 1996   57405'26322—dc20
95-36228   CIP
                                                            AC

ISBN 0–8050–4089–7
First Edition—1996

Cover design by Betty Lew
Interior design by Kelly Soong

Photo credits appear on page 78.

CONTENTS

INTRODUCTION
TO AQUATIC BIOMES

The water that makes up more than two-thirds of your body weight, that flows in your blood, that bathes your cells, and that you cry as tears, may once have flowed in a river. It may have floated as a cloud, fallen as a snowflake, bobbed in ocean waves, or been drunk by a dinosaur from an ancient lake. All this is possible because the water that's presently on earth has always been here—except for ice brought by comets hitting the earth's atmosphere. And all the water on earth is connected in a global cycle. This cycle is called the water cycle, or the hydrologic cycle.

Every day, all over the earth, water exists in and moves through this cycle. Ninety-seven percent of the earth's water is in the oceans. Two percent is in frozen glaciers and ice caps at the Poles. The remaining 1 percent is divided among the world's lakes, rivers, groundwater, soil moisture, and water vapor in the air. All this comes to a grand total of 326 million cubic miles (1,359 million cubic kilometers) of water. Every day, this water is exchanged among the oceans, streams, clouds, glaciers, lakes, wetlands, and even dew-covered leaves. Even now, it is being exhaled from your body, as moisture in your breath.

As the water cycles, at times it changes phase from solid to liquid to gas. The heat of the sun warms water on the land's surface, in lakes, in streams, in the ocean, even on the leaves of plants—and causes this water to evaporate, to turn into a gas. This gas rises into the air, cools, and condenses, eventually forming clouds and falling back to earth as liquid rain or solid snow or hail. This precipitation makes its way into streams, rivers, lakes, oceans, glaciers, and ice caps, and underground. And so the cycle continues. But it's not quite so simple. Each portion of the cycle is connected to others. For example, river water runs into oceans, stream water runs into lakes, and water from underground bubbles out of springs and into rivers. Water is constantly being exchanged among all the many places it resides on planet earth.

Almost anywhere water exists as a liquid, it is colonized by organisms—bacteria, amoebas, fungi, animals, or plants. Some watery habitats have particular physical conditions and particular kinds of plants and animals inhabiting them. These are aquatic biomes: ocean, river, lake, and coral reef. Where these aquatic biomes mingle with terrestrial, or land, biomes, they may form special, semiaquatic, fringe communities. Wetland and seashore are two of these communities that are unique enough and widespread enough to qualify as major biomes.

All aquatic and semiaquatic biomes—ocean, river, lake, coral reef, seashore, and wetland—are influenced by regional climate and the lands nearby. These biomes are also linked to one another, by ever-moving water molecules and the global water cycle through which they flow.

❧ 1 ❧
THE LAKE AND POND BIOME

If you're searching for ponds and lakes, look and listen for the animals. At dusk, follow the V-shaped flocks of migrating geese. In spring, listen for the chirping, burping calls of frogs as they chorus, advertising their prowess and their pond. Keep an eye out for clouds of midges, trees gnawed by beavers, or wood ducks dropping low, with whistling wings. If all else fails, follow the person with the fishing pole, or the car with the sailboat towed behind.

Lakes and ponds are still-water habitats. They don't gurgle, rush, and run as rivers do. They're settling places, where rivers drop their load of silt, where water running off the land ends up. Lakes and ponds are environments that host tiny, floating organisms that cannot survive a river's flow. And they're relatively short-lived habitats, in geologic time. Over thousands or even hundreds of years, most fill with sediment and decayed plants and animals, eventually becoming dry land.

A few lakes are so tremendous, they're in a class by themselves. Siberia's Lake Baikal has existed for twenty-five million years. It's the world's oldest, deepest lake, plunging 1 mile (1.6 kilometers) deep, and holding one-fifth of the fresh water on earth. The Caspian Sea—which is a lake despite its name—is bordered by the former Soviet states and is home to seals, sturgeon, and sponges. (The Caspian Sea has a surface area larger than Italy!) And North America's Great Lakes have waves, storms, and ship-wrecks, making them seem more like oceans than lakes.

Together, lakes and ponds form a biome, an area that has a certain kind of community of animals and plants. The lake biome is aquatic—a water biome. And it's a freshwater biome, meaning its water is generally not as salty as the ocean. (Although some salt lakes are an exception to this rule.) Unlike terrestrial biomes, such as grassland, desert, and tundra, the lake biome does not have a characteristic climate. It is strongly affected by whatever terrestrial biome surrounds it.

Two main kinds of lake dominate the earth: freshwater lakes, and salt and soda lakes. The water in freshwater lakes is relatively pure, compared to the chemical-laden water of salt and soda lakes. Salt and soda lakes such as the Caspian Sea, Utah's Great Salt Lake, and the Dead Sea between Jordan and Israel, create chemically harsh conditions for aquatic life. Yet those species that do survive in these lakes

A gull feasts on brine flies on the shore of Mono Lake, California.

Calcium carbonate deposits called tufa towers form a dramatic background for several gulls. Soon these gulls will be joined by thousands of other birds that feed and nest at Mono Lake.

thrive in staggering numbers. Every year, California's Mono Lake hosts hundreds of thousands of birds that feed on a sun-warmed feast of shrimp and flies. Africa's Lake Tanganyika is carpeted with pink—pink flamingos, that is.

Lakes are not plentiful on every continent. South America, for instance, has relatively few. Much of its land is drained by rivers that feed into the Amazon River. And most of its land was never covered by glaciers that helped form the lake-filled landscapes of the northern portions of North America, Europe, and Asia. Africa, although untouched by glaciers, has an abundance of large lakes, including Lake Tanganyika, Lake Albert, and Lake Nyasa. These lakes lie in a mammoth geological crevice called the Great Rift Valley.

This book concentrates on lakes in North America, in particular, the lakes of the temperate zone. These lakes and ponds are magnets for wildlife: places where fish swim, beavers build, and dragonflies dance. Loons use these lakes as stages for courtship rituals. Moose dive down deeply to munch on plants. Lakes and ponds are critical to the lives of these wild animals, and for people, too.

TYPES

There are two main types of lake:
- Freshwater lakes, which contain only trace amounts of chemicals.
- Salt and soda lakes, which contain high concentrations of salts and carbonates, respectively.

DIVISIONS

Lakes have two major life zones:
- The euphotic zone—the zone where light penetrates.
- The profundal zone, which receives 1 percent or less of the sunlight from the surface.

Lakes are also divided into layers according to temperature and water density.

PHYSICAL FEATURES

Lakes and ponds generally have the following features:
- Little water flow, compared to rivers.
- Fresh water (except in salt lakes).
- Impermanence: over centuries or millennia, they fill with sediment and eventually become dry land.
- In the case of deep lakes, stratification—layers of water of different temperatures that form in summer.

ANIMALS

- Insect larvae, worms, and snails live in the lake bottom, surviving on food dropping from above.
- Lakes have fewer animal species than are found in rivers.
- Zooplankton—tiny floating animals—that feed on algae are abundant.
- Fish are generally the largest carnivores, although there may be land-based carnivores such as birds.

- Some aquatic species can enter a resting stage, called diapause, in winter or when the pool dries up, then return to active life when conditions improve.

PLANTS

- The bulk of the plants are phytoplankton—tiny green algae, diatoms, and cyanobacteria—that float in the water.
- Macrophytes—larger plants—grow out from the shores.
- Plants are adapted to avoid sinking down, out of the range of sunlight.

2

NORTH AMERICAN
LAKES AND PONDS

Flying over North America, you can see it's a continent rich
with lakes. From the air, they look like mirrors or shiny foil.
They sparkle in Louisiana's lowlands, dot the prairies of the
Dakotas, and form pockets of blue in Canada's green North
Woods. Lake waters lap Chicago's Lake Shore Drive, reflect
Rocky Mountain peaks, and fleck Mexico's Sonora Desert
after heavy rains. All over the continent, lakes and ponds
hold water for fish, birds, and humans, too.

Glaciers—mile-thick rivers of slow-moving ice—once
covered much of Canada, Alaska, and northern states such
as Michigan, Minnesota, Wisconsin, and Maine. The ice left
lakes as a legacy, through processes that will be described in
chapter 3. Minnesota, whose motto is "The land of 10,000
lakes," is actually modest in its claims. Only lakes 25 acres
(10 hectares) or more in size were counted; there are
thousands of smaller ones as well. Canada also has a lake-
speckled landscape, with notable lakes such as Lake
Winnipeg, Great Slave Lake, and Great Bear Lake. In addition, it also shares shores of the Great Lakes with its neigh-
bor, the United States.

These glaciated regions have the highest concentration
of lakes. But North America has spectacular lakes elsewhere, too. In Oregon, the collapsed cone of a volcano holds

Glaciers similar to the Worthington Glacier in Alaska help create lakes across the northern portion of North America.

Crater Lake. In Utah's desert, brine shrimp wriggle in the Great Salt Lake. Along the Gulf Coast of Texas and Mexico, birds by the thousands feed in seaside lakes called lagoons. And in mountains near Mexico City, rivers flow not seaward, but into massive inland lakes.

North America also has uncounted thousands of artificial lakes and ponds. People create them to help wildlife, to water cattle, and to raise fish. Lakes are also made for reservoirs to store drinking water and as a by-product of building dams.

THE GREAT LAKES

Perhaps the most remarkable of North America's lakes are its five Great Lakes: Superior, Michigan, Ontario, Huron, and Erie. These lakes cover 95,000 square miles (247,000

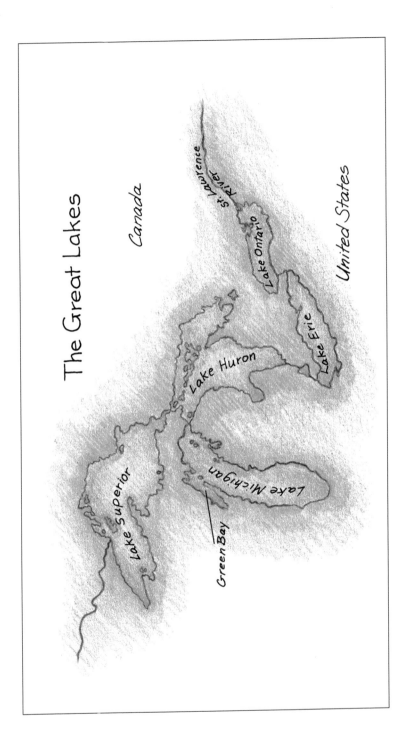

The Great Lakes

Canada

United States

St. Lawrence River

Lake Ontario

Lake Erie

Lake Huron

Lake Superior

Lake Michigan

Green Bay

square kilometers)—the biggest area of fresh water on earth. One-fifth of the world's fresh water is held between these shores. Yet the lakes are comparatively shallow, except for Lake Superior, which reaches 1,300 feet (396 meters) deep.

The Great Lakes are the site of major shipping channels because they're connected to one another and to the sea. Water flows from Lake Superior and Lake Michigan into Lake Huron then through Lake Erie and Lake Ontario, out through the St. Lawrence River to the Atlantic Ocean. This is one reason the lakes are the site of major cities such as Chicago and Detroit. Lake barges distribute products from heavy shoreline industry and from farm fields farther inland.

The Great Lakes drain rivers from Montana to New York. But their drainage area is small compared to their size. River water and groundwater contribute only a portion of the lake's water. Rain and snow falling on their surface provide half of the supply.

Over these lakes, air masses clash, forming ferocious storms. And winds whip up gigantic waves. Lake waters can slosh back and forth, in surges covering hundreds of miles. Fierce storms can cause shipwrecks, such as the wreck of forty ships in 1913, and the downing of the famous *Edmund Fitzgerald* in 1975. And in places, waves and currents eat away at the shore, causing roads and houses to fall into the lakes.

The Great Lakes strongly influence people's lives. They are important for wildlife, recreation, fishing, swimming, and industry. Their vast bulk of water even affects the weather. They are truly North America's inland seas.

❦ 3 ❧
PHYSICAL FEATURES OF LAKES AND PONDS

If you want to know what a lake bottom looks like, take a look at the surrounding land. Steep-sided mountains surround steep-sided lakes. Smooth, gentle hills surround gently sloped ponds. Land shapes a lake's contours and chemistry. Yet the lake affects the land, in turn. It can bring cooler summers, warmer winters, and harsh blizzards to lands nearby.

LAKE BASICS

A pond is a small, shallow body of water. Lakes tend to be larger and deeper. Ponds tend to be shallow enough so that light can reach their bottom. Rooted plants can grow shore to shore. Lakes are large enough to have windswept shores and deep enough to form summertime layers of cold and warm water. But which characteristic is more important is debatable. Even limnologists—scientists who study lakes and ponds—don't agree on the exact difference between the two!

Water Sources   The basins of lakes and ponds get their water from many sources, including rivers, rain, and melting snow. Water running off the land, seeping from the ground, and melting off glaciers fills them, too. Each lake or pond may have one or more water source. Many lakes are associated with rivers. A lake may be the beginning of a river or the place a river ends. A lake can also occur along a river's length, where river water slows and puddles for a while, before rushing on.

Many Chemistries   Whether a lake is clear, cloudy, salty, acidic, or polluted, its chemistry depends on its water sources and the underlying rock that forms its basin. A muddy river forms a muddy lake. River water and rainwater running over rocks can pick up natural salts and carry them into lakes. When rivers pour into lakes, their water slows down and drops much of its load of silt. As a result, river water that leaves a lake tends to be cleaner than the river water that entered it.

Settle Down and Concentrate!   Whatever is carried by water into a lake tends to build up in a lake over time. As water evaporates from a lake's surface, it leaves its dissolved chemicals behind. These chemicals can become concentrated in the remaining water, more and more over the years. Some lakes become so salty they're classified as salt lakes; others build up carbonates and are termed soda lakes.

Catch a Wave!   Lakes are windy places. Wind blowing across a lake's surface can pick up speed, without trees or obstacles in the way. Wind whips up waves and creates currents that push against the lakeshore. Strong winds and changes in air pressure can create tidelike surges called seiches. A seiche occurs when water piles up at one end of a lake, then flows back to the other end. The water continues rocking back and forth, like water sloshing in a bowl. Seiches on Lake Erie can cause water at one end of the lake to be more than 13 feet (4 meters) higher than at the other end! Boat operators plan their routes to avoid these dangerous seiches.

Lakes are often windy, making them great places to windsurf!

Changing Shorelines Like ocean waves and currents, lake waves and currents can move sand, mud, and silt from place to place. This naturally erodes—carries away—land from one part of the lake and deposits it in another. Parts of the Great Lakes' shoreline—primarily the northern Wisconsin coast of Lake Superior, the southern shore of Lake Erie, and the eastern shore of Lake Michigan—are naturally eroding. During big storms, houses sometimes fall into the lakes.

LAKE LAYERS

How well lake waters mix, bottom to top, makes a big difference in plants' and animals' lives. It determines whether oxygen and minerals can circulate, nourishing organisms and keeping them alive. Like oil-and-vinegar salad dressing, some lakes stratify—forming layers that prevent water from mixing thoroughly. In the temperate zone of North America, mixing and layering occur seasonally.

The Layered Look: Summer In summer, deep lakes form layers. Sun and warm air heat water near the surface. But farther down, the water remains cool. Cold, dense water

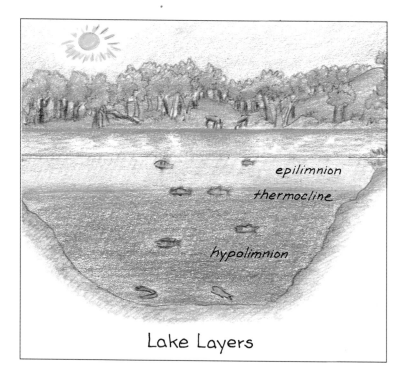

Lake Layers

moves to the bottom of the lake, forming a layer called the hypolimnion. Warmer water, which is less dense, floats on top, forming the epilimnion. In between is a transition zone, the thermocline, where temperature changes quickly with depth.

Seasonal Changes In autumn, the top layer of water loses heat, and lake layers dissipate. Strong winds mix the water thoroughly. But over the winter, the lake stratifies again. Cold air cools the surface water, while deeper waters remain relatively warm. Ice forms, preventing wind mixing. So the layers remain until spring, when the ice melts and wind mixes the lake water again.

More Mixed-up Lakes Twice a year, the mixing described in this section occurs in temperate lakes, such as those in

North America. Tropical lakes may mix more or less often. And not all lakes stratify. Ponds and shallow lakes, for instance, may be constantly mixed by wind. The surface waters of cold, iced-over lakes in the Arctic and alpine regions may never warm up enough to stratify at all.

LAKESIDE WEATHER

"Lake-effect snow on the way," proclaims the weather report in Benton Harbor, Michigan. Like many large lakes, Lake Michigan affects the weather for miles around.

Mild Seasons The reason lakes affect local weather is that water warms up more slowly and cools off more slowly than air. In summer, lake waters still cool from winter and spring can help keep surrounding air cool. Wind may carry this cool air inland, creating a cool lake breeze. In winter, a lake only slowly cools off. So its warmth may make winter slightly warmer nearby.

Lake-Effect Snows In winter, air flowing across a large lake can pick up moisture. Then, near the lake's edge, the warm moisture hits cold air that hangs over the land. This clash of warm and cold air creates snow called lake-effect snow. Lake effect brings heavy snowfall—an average of 85 inches (216 centimeters) of snow a year—to Buffalo, New York, on the eastern shore of Lake Erie. Lake-effect snows drop even more impressive amounts on towns of the Keweenaw Peninsula of Michigan and Boonville, Bennett Bridge, and other New York towns of the Tug Hill Plateau at the eastern end of Lake Ontario. These places, which proudly compete for the distinction of snowiest place east of the Rockies, receive more than 200 inches (500 centimeters) of snow on average, and a whopping 300 to 400 inches (760 to 1,020 centimeters) in their snowiest years.

LAKE BASINS: THEY'RE THE PITS

Any natural force that creates large pits in the earth's surface can create a basin where a lake may form. Swirling winds blow away sand or soil, creating low-lying spots that fill with rain. A volcano, after eruption, can collapse in upon itself, forming a caldera that will hold a lake. Underground rivers can dissolve rock, creating caverns that collapse, leaving sinkhole lakes. Even a meteorite hitting the earth can make a hole, such as New Quebec Crater, where a Canadian lake formed.

*Lake-effect snows cause dramatic amounts of
snowfall in some areas bordering the Great Lakes.*

Cracks and Crevices   Pieces of the earth's crust are constantly rising, falling, wrinkling, stretching, and pushing against one another in some places, and pulling apart in others. Where the land pulls apart, deep rifts called grabens may form. Water fills some of these rifts creating lakes such as California's scenic Lake Tahoe and Siberia's 1-mile- (1.6-kilometer-) deep Lake Baikal.

Puddles of the Sea   Over thousands of years, the world's sea level rises and falls, according to the climate. At one time, the sea flooded much of Florida. But later it retreated, leaving giant puddles of seawater that became Lake Okeechobee, Lake Apopka, and Lake Weir. The Caspian Sea and the Aral Sea between Kazakhstan and Uzbekistan in the former Soviet Union also formed this way.

Re-formed Rivers   Block a river's flow and what you make is a lake. Landslides, lava flows, windblown sand, coastal sandspits, and glacial debris can all help block rivers, forming lakes. Rivers can also overflow their banks,

*High in the Sierra Nevada lies
Lake Tahoe, an exceptionally deep lake.*

forming shallow floodplain lakes. (The Amazon, when it floods, forms more than 8,000 lakes, some of which are several miles long.) And tightly looping rivers can jump their banks and change course, abandoning old river loops that become oxbow lakes. (These lakes are named for their bow-like shapes.)

Rivers of Ice   In northern regions, glaciers formed most of the lake basins. Several times over tens of thousands of years, these gigantic rivers of ice pushed their way south, scouring the land as they went. Glaciers helped form lakes in many ways. They deepened and widened river valleys; left piles of rubble, called moraines, which blocked river valleys; and pressed down the land, which later rose up and tilted as the glaciers retreated. All these processes helped form the Great Lakes and other smaller lakes. These lakes

Day after day, year after year, mud and other particles settle to the bottom of a lake. Pollen grains, leaves, shells, bones, and other materials are deposited, too. Over time, these sediments become a pile of clues, a layer cake of information about the past life of the lake. Scientists called paleolimnologists study this record by drilling down into the lake sediment. They pull out cylinders of sediment, called cores. Then they study these mud cores to learn about the past. By examining the remains of ancient animals and pollen grains in lower layers, scientists can find out what animals and plants lived in and around the lake thousands of years ago.

Cores of lake sediment can provide valuable information.

run generally north to south and fan out, as the glacier's ice sheets once did.

Meltwater Lakes   Mixed in with the silt dropped by glaciers were giant blocks of ice. When these ice blocks melted, they left small basins that later filled with water, forming lakes, ponds, and wetlands. These basins, called kettles or prairie potholes, dot North America's prairies by the thousands.

Living Lake Makers   Beavers and people are prodigious lake makers. Beavers dam streams to create deep ponds

But how do scientists know how long ago each layer was deposited? The bottom layers are the oldest. Layers near the top are more recent. For measurements in more recent times, in temperate regions of the earth, paleolimnologists can count layers year by year. Each year two distinguishable layers are deposited on the lake bottom. A layer of coarse particles settles out in spring. A layer of finer particles settles out as the lake freezes in winter.

Estimating the age of older layers, which have been pressed down together for hundreds or thousands of years, can be more difficult. Additional clues are needed. Paleolimnologists can tell the age of certain layers and use them as markers. The year of a volcanic eruption, for instance, will have a higher concentration of ash. Layers after the industrial revolution contain lead, which is emitted by air-polluting factories and settles in lakes around the world. By measuring distances from these known layers, scientists can estimate the age of the rest of the core.

where they build their lodges. People bulldoze pits to create ponds to water livestock, to raise fish, and to attract wildlife. People also dam rivers, which creates huge lakes, and mine rock, leaving holes that fill with rain, creating quarry lakes. Some of these lakes and ponds support fish and other creatures and become integral to the surrounding landscape.

25

LAKE AND POND PLANTS

To grow and make food through photosynthesis, plants need water, minerals, and sunlight. Water is no problem in a lake, of course. Mineral availability varies from lake to lake. Sunlight is available near the surface—in the euphotic zone. This zone, the light-filled layer, may reach 165 feet (50 meters) down in clear lakes. In muddy lakes, sunlight may penetrate only 20 inches (51 centimeters) or so. Either way, the euphotic zone remains the layer of life, below which plants, sunlight-starved, will die.

PLANT ADAPTATIONS

The main plants in lakes and ponds are so small you might not even notice they're there, at first. These plant phytoplankton. Many are micro different species and shapes. G dots, or long strings of conne diatoms have intricate shells made move through the water with tiny component of phytoplankton, once and considered a plant, is now rena classified with bacteria instead!

Not Just for Ducks Floating on the and ponds are tiny plants the size of le

26

a favorite food for ducks, hence their name, duckweed. Intermixed with duckweed are even smaller plants called watermeal. Watermeal and duckweed are worth a closer look; they bear some of the smallest flowering plants on earth. Duckweed floats on a pond's surface during spring and summer. But late in the season, it produces an excess of starch, becoming so heavy it sinks to the bottom. During the winter, however, it uses this food to stay alive. So by spring it's light again, and it floats back up to the water's surface, coating the pond with green.

Both frogs and duckweed can be found in many lakes and ponds.

The Big Stuff Ponds and lakes also contain bigger aquatic plants, which scientists term macrophytes. Macrophytes include large algae, mosses, and flowering plants. Cattails, reeds, water lilies, milfoil, bladderworts, water willow, and buttonbush are some of the common species. Like animals, these plants need oxygen for their cells to respire. It helps them use the food they make to keep their cells alive. But underwater, in mud, oxygen can be scarce, so plants pump oxygen from surface leaves to their roots. For this reason, their leaves and stems may be spongy and filled with air. Underwater, some mosquito larvae even tap into plant stems for air, so they won't need to surface for a breath!

That Sinking Feeling   For aquatic plants, a major challenge is staying near the surface, where light is plentiful. Spines increase the surface area of tiny phytoplankton, helping them to stay afloat. Dinoflagellates actively swim to stay afloat—certainly a strange habit for plants! Water lilies' leaves float flat on the water's surface. (Long, flexible stems allow them to rise and fall with changing water levels.) And other plants have balloonlike, air-filled stem swellings, which are used as flotation devices.

To Root or Not to Root   On land, roots not only anchor plants but help them to take up water and minerals as well. In still-water habitats, plants are bathed in water containing minerals, and they don't always need anchoring. So roots often play less of a role. Milfoil and hornwort float freely, never rooting at all. Water hyacinths have roots that trail down but don't hold them in place. Near shore, there are rooted plants such as cattails and reeds.

What About Sex?   For plants, "sex" is exchanging pollen to make seeds. How water plants do this is quite remarkable. Hornworts' pollen packets float to the water's surface. There they burst, the pollen flies out, and sinks down to pollinate underwater flowers. Water soldier plants send flowers to the surface, where the rotten-smelling flowers attract flies. The flies, fooled into thinking there's a rotten-meat feast, fly from flower to flower, pollinating them. Sexual reproduction isn't necessary every time. Aquatic macrophytes can reproduce another way. Reaching roots and broken-off bits of stems may grow into new plants. Unlike plants from seeds, these new plants are clones—genetically identical to the original plant.

PLANT WORLD

Plants are more than just food for animals. The way plants grow shapes the life of the pond. Large aquatic plants host a whole slimy community of life: of algae, one-celled creatures, and detritus. Germans call this slime layer *Aufwuchs*—a name that sounds fitting for the way this material feels. Its sliminess comes from algae, which secrete soft wet coverings. The other material just gets stuck. Snails graze on this *Aufwuchs,* as on peanut butter, scraping it up with their toothed tongues. Plants not only support this living slime but can change the aquatic environment over time. Their growth can cover a lake or fill in a pond, as we'll see in chapter 6.

❧ 5 ❧
LAKE AND POND
ANIMALS

You probably won't find a monster in a lake, even if you search Scotland's Loch Ness. But you will find zooplankton—tiny floating animals, rather monsterlike, although miniature in form. Zooplankton called daphnia swim in sudden, jerky motions, catching food morsels with the hair on their legs. Microscopic rotifers use crowns of hairlike cilia to sweep algae directly to their mouths. Bigger animals—beavers, herons, and fish—stay busy gnawing, spearing, and gulping food. Tiny flatworms make their way from snail to swimmer, where they'll settle in and make somebody itch.

AQUATIC ANIMAL ADAPTATIONS

How do you avoid predators if you're a tiny floating food morsel? Be transparent. The bodies of daphnia and numerous other zooplankton are. This is only one of many ways lake and pond animals are adapted for aquatic life. Zooplankton are still vulnerable to predators because their dark eyes and food-filled guts give away their location. So, to further avoid predators, they migrate down into the lake's depths in daytime. But at night they migrate back upward to feed on phytoplankton, which stay near the surface.

It's Raining Food   In the dim depths of lakes is a plantless world. Creatures there eat animals that swim down from upper layers. Or they dine on what falls from above: detritus—bits of plants, decaying algae, droppings, and other tidbits. Mussels siphon in water and filter out food particles. Worms find food in mud and sand. Other creatures specialize in eating one another—and have to find their prey in the dark!

Complicated Lives   Many aquatic insects have a bottom-dwelling phase but spend the rest of their lives elsewhere in lakes. Mosquitoes, midges, blackflies, dragonflies, and mayflies all start life as eggs. They hatch into underwater

Dragonfly eggs hatch into underwater larvae.

This green darner dragonfly has just emerged from its larval skin.

Adult green darner dragonflies may live for only a short season.

larvae that live for several months or years on rocks, on the lake bottom, or among plants. Only later do they molt and/or pass through a pupal stage and live as winged adults, for a few short hours, days, or weeks. Adult midges and mayflies don't even eat. They just mate, lay eggs, and die.

Swimmer's Itch   During and after a swim in a lake, you may feel itchy and develop small, red spots. What you have is swimmer's itch. Tiny flatworms have penetrated your skin. More often, they infect muskrat or ducks. But inside a human, duck, or muskrat body, the flatworm larvae attach to blood vessels in the intestine. Their eggs travel out of the body in feces. Then they hatch into wiggling larvae that seek out aquatic snails. Inside snails, the larvae transform once again, to become the mobile larvae that cause swimmer's itch. In tropical countries, other flatworms with similar life cycles cause deadly diseases such as schistosomiasis.

LIFE IN A DROP OF WATER

Find out what microscopic creatures live in lake and pond waters.

Materials you'll need:
- Several small jars with lids for collecting water
- Water dropper
- Microscope
- Slides and cover slips
- Water life guidebook (optional—used for identifying microscopic creatures)

1. In the lidded jars, collect water samples from nearby lakes and ponds. About ½ cup (240 milliliters) of water from each source should be plenty.

2. Use a dropper to place a tiny water droplet on a slide. Cover with a cover slip.

3. Examine the slide under the microscope. Focus in and out to find the creatures at different levels in the water.

4. Count, draw, and describe the organisms you see. If you have a lab book or water-life guidebook, identify the organisms. You're likely to find diatoms, strings of algae, paramecia, stentors, amoebas, volvox, daphnia, rotifers, and other organisms.

5. Examine several different samples. Are there any differences between the samples from different ponds and lakes? What do you think accounts for such differences?

Some Things Fishy Fish have many adaptations for living underwater. They extract air from water by gulping it in their mouths and pumping the water over their gills. Blood vessels close to the surface of the gills take in needed oxygen from this water and dump carbon dioxide—a waste product—into it as well. The water is then pushed out of the fish's gill slits, the crescent-shaped openings on each side of its head. In addition to gills, fish have other adaptations, such as swim bladders. A swim bladder is a balloonlike organ. It helps keep the fish buoyant as it swims. The fish can add air to or withdraw air from its swim bladder in order to change how high in the water it floats.

Fish Dinners Fish can eat a whole range of foods. But many species specialize in what they eat and where they dine. Bluegill feed on insect larvae. Crappies dine on tiny zooplankton. And pumpkinseed crush snails in their teeth. Golden shiners and sunfish swim the surface of ponds, whereas bullheads and darters roam the bottom. Some fish change locations during the day. Many move to the surface to feed in the evening. That's a good time for feeding, because insects are active and zooplankton are rising to the surface for the night.

Stay in School!   Many fish school—swim together in coordinated groups—because they're less likely to be eaten that way. More fish mean more eyes to look for predators. And from a distance, a school of fish may look like one giant fish, instead of many bite-size ones. Predators also have a difficult time selecting which fish to chase, especially in the confusion as a school darts away.

VISITORS AND EDGE-DWELLERS

Many lake and pond inhabitants live double lives, sharing their time between water and land. Kingfishers perch in trees, then dive in to catch fish. Salamanders and frogs live on land, but require water where they can lay their eggs and their young can develop.

Ah, The Smell of Pond Scum   In spring, male and female wood frogs return to the pond where they hatched. They find it by its distinctive smell. There male wood frogs gather with male frogs of many other species to chorus—to call to attract females to their "pad." Frog calls vary. Spring peepers chirp. Pig frogs grunt like their namesakes—pigs. And chorus frogs sound distinctly like a finger running along the teeth of a comb. When the male frogs have attracted the females, the females lay eggs, which the males fertilize. The hatched eggs become tadpoles, which live for a while in water, then develop and hop away as frogs.

Birds and More Birds   Not just ducks but many other wild birds utilize lakes and ponds. Long-legged herons and limpkins wade in the water, spearing and snatching fish with their bills. Cuckoos, flycatchers, warblers, and other insect eaters catch flying insects emerging from their aquatic stage. Osprey search for fish from their perches, then glide in and grasp them in their talons. And loons dive deeply, pursuing fish who try to dart away.

Beavers: The Builders Beavers build dams across brooks and streams to create the deep-water habitats they prefer. They cut down trees and gather sticks, and construct stick-and-mud dams up to 10 feet (3 meters) high and 2,000 feet (610 meters) long. Beavers continually repair their dams. The sound of flowing water stimulates them to patch the holes. Waterproof fur, webbed feet, and wide, mud-packing tails all make beavers suited for their lifestyle. A beaver's four front teeth—two bottom and two top—grow out in front of its lips. That way its lips can close behind its teeth so it won't get water or wood chips in its mouth when it gnaws. Unlike people's incisors, a beaver's four incisors keep growing, pushing upward, all through its life. This replaces the tooth surfaces worn away as the beaver gnaws on wood.

Watch a beaver for a while, and you will understand the origin of the expression "busy as a beaver"!

· DUCK LOVERS, UNITE! ·

Look out on a lake and you're likely to see ducks. Get hold of binoculars and you're in for a treat, because ducks are a colorful, entertaining bunch. Buffleheads, their white crests flared, bob and dive. Northern shovelers tip up, tails afloat. Mallards and black ducks search the shore for seeds.

Ducks vary in their feeding styles. Dabbling ducks, such as pintails, mallards, teals, and shovelers, stay on the surface, dipping their bills and shaking their heads. A comblike edge on their bill sifts food particles—seeds, insects, and duckweed—from the water. Diving ducks, such as redheads, scaups, and mergansers, swim in deeper waters, disappearing now and then. They dive deeply to capture fish before returning to the surface for air.

One of the most exciting times to see ducks is when they are migrating in spring and fall. Thousands of ducks and geese gather on lakes to rest and feed during their journey. Look for them late in the day as they fly in to settle down before dark. To learn more about the birds in your area, contact your local chapter of the Audubon Society. Audubon members often take beginning bird-watchers out to see the sights.

Water Safety   The middle of a lake or pond can be a safe haven where animals escape terrestrial predators such as bobcats, coyotes, and wolves. Once beavers have dammed a stream, creating a pond, they build lodges—conical piles of sticks—with underwater entrances where they can quickly retreat. (Muskrat build similar but smaller lodges.) At night, gulls and ducks sleep in the middle of lakes to avoid predators that prowl the shores. And because of their built-in "moats," islands within lakes are popular nesting sites for birds.

LAKE AND POND IN WINTER

What happens to lake and pond dwellers when winter comes and the water begins to freeze? Duckweed sinks to the lake bottom. Plants form seeds or die back to their roots. Many birds migrate south to lakes that aren't covered with ice. Other animals, however, remain in the freezing lake landscape, so they have to be adapted to cope with cold.

Thank a Water Molecule   Thanks to a peculiar property of water, most lakes don't freeze solid in winter. When water freezes, it forms a crystalline structure that is less dense than liquid water. So ice floats on liquid water. If ice did not float, it would sink to the bottom as it formed. Cold air over the lake would cool the surface waters, forming more ice that would sink, and so on. Eventually, the whole lake would freeze solid, bottom to top. And fish could not survive.

No Frozen Fish Section   As it is, however, the lake ice floats. It insulates the water underneath from the cold air above. This helps keep the water somewhat warm and habitable for fish and other creatures. Using light that penetrates thin lake ice, a few plants can still photosynthesize. But if snow covers the ice, blocking the light, the plants cannot produce food and oxygen, a by-product of photosynthesis. As a result, in winter months, oxygen can become scarce as animals use it up. Fish crowd close to ice holes, where oxygen is more plentiful. If the oxygen becomes really scarce, some fish may die. In spring, you may see the dead bodies of these fish floating on the surface of the lake.

Weird Wood Frogs In winter, wood frogs freeze solid and stiff. Their lungs stop working. They no longer move. The secret to their survival is glucose concentrated in their bodies. Glucose prevents ice crystals from forming, expanding, and rupturing cells. So when warm weather comes, the frogs thaw and hop to the closest pond. Most other frogs and turtles spend their winters hibernating deep in mud. They slow down their bodily functions, and their temperatures drop, so they don't move much until they've warmed for spring.

Time Capsules In lakes and ponds, many microscopic animals and plants die when the winter comes. But some survive in special forms. Freshwater sponges form hard-walled cysts. Hydras produce embryos in hard casings. Freshwater jellyfish create a protective coat. Water fleas lay

Wood frogs spend the winter frozen solid.
They thaw out in spring.

special, thick-walled eggs. These forms help organisms survive the cold.

Laying Low   Aquatic insects such as whirligigs, diving beetles, back swimmers, and water boatmen hibernate under leaves, in plant stems, and in mud and sand. Midges and mayflies survive as eggs. Mussels and clams enter a resting stage, called diapause, with little activity or growth. Dragonfly and damselfly larvae live through the winter, although they are less active in these months.

The Active Ones   Muskrat and beavers are active in winter. They feed from winter caches of food: leafy plants, small tree shoots, and bark stashed underwater. They may also swim and look for food under the ice, or crawl out of cracks in the ice and search the shores.

Ponds in winter can be quiet places—icy and beautiful.

The Winter Scene On warm days in winter, muskrat and other pond animals may be active. You might see them wandering the shores. But overall, in winter, the pond is a quiet place. It's as if the world is waiting for the ice to thaw.

❦ 6 ❦
THE LAKE AND POND COMMUNITY

Don't judge a book just by its cover, or a lake by its color alone, because appearances can be deceiving. A clear blue lake that seems beautiful may be polluted and biologically dead. A brown, muddy pond full of stumps, sticks, and plants may seem messy but be healthy and full of fish. To truly evaluate the health of a lake or pond, scientists must get beyond color and get up close. They must understand the lake's or pond's physical features and its living community of animals and plants.

ENERGY AT WORK

One day in a green pond, a tiny plant was eaten by a tiny copepod, which was eaten by a fish, which was eaten by a bigger fish, which was eaten by a long-legged bird. This short story describes a food chain—a series of plants and animals linked by what they eat. Several food chains linked together become a food web, which shows relationships among many organisms in a community.

High Energy   Who eats what and who eats whom is not just about food. It's about energy. In a pond, energy from the sun is stored by phytoplankton—plants—in the molecules that make up their tissues. Part of this energy becomes

In this lake food chain, energy from the sun passes to tiny organisms near the start of the chain. Eventually, some of that same energy will flow to a bald eagle, a top predator.

part of the copepod that eats the phytoplankton. Part of the copepod's energy becomes part of the fish that eats it. And so on, and so on, energy passes along the food chain. But some of it is used up during the daily activity of organisms, and some of it is dissipated as heat. That's why energy is lost at every stage where it's transferred, such as when one organism is eaten by another.

The Power of Pyramids   It takes many phytoplankton to feed a copepod, and many copepods to feed a fish. And it takes many fish to feed a blue heron, a top predator. Ecologists, scientists who study natural communities, describe these relationships as an energy pyramid. Top predators, who eat animals supported by many food-web

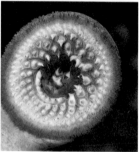

Lampreys have attached themselves to this carp, using mouths like suction cups and sharp horned teeth (inset).

links, tend to be rare. Part of the reason is that energy is lost at every link. That's one reason plants, which form the base of the pyramid, must be plentiful for a healthy ecosystem, and its top predators, to survive. All the organisms are connected in a community; their fates are intertwined. In lakes and ponds, tiny, barely visible phytoplankton are the main organisms that form the energy pyramid's base.

EXOTIC SPECIES

Sometime in the 1800s, a blood-drinking, flesh-eating sea creature called the sea lamprey entered the Great Lakes. It latched onto fish, weakening or killing them, and leading to many species' decline. This nonnative, exotic animal

· MUSSEL POWER! ·

What is car-shaped, is covered with a three-inch layer of mussels, and used to be red? A Camaro the Canadian police pulled from Lake Erie in 1989. After just eight months underwater, the red Camaro was covered with zebra mussels, all the way from its bumpers to its seat belts. The "mussel car," as it was

It takes only a few zebra mussels to begin a colony.

nicknamed, illustrated what biologists already knew: zebra mussels will stick to just about anything. Like barnacles, zebra mussels are fouling organisms—they stick to boats, slowing them down; ruin fishing nets; clog the insides of boat engines; and block water intake pipes used by towns and industry. Basically, zebra mussels foul things up. And chances are they're coming to a lake or stream near you.

Zebra mussels are an exotic species, not native to North America. Sometime in 1985 or 1986, the zebra mussel was brought into the Great Lakes, probably in the ballast water of a

changed the food web dramatically. Often, exotic species do so by endangering or competing with native animals and native plants. Since the 1800s, 139 exotic species, from fish to diatoms to mussels, have taken hold in the Great Lakes.

Dumping Grounds   How do exotic species get into lakes and ponds? Some are released by fishery managers on purpose, in order to satisfy fishermen's desire for certain

European freighter. Since that time, the mussel has spread through the Great Lakes, into the Mississippi River, all the way to New Orleans. It's even been found in isolated lakes such as Wawasee Lake, Indiana, where it spread on boats taken from lake to lake.

A similar effect is expected in other lakes. And boy, can these creatures "mussel in." Biologists counted 1,000 zebra mussels in one square meter area, then recounted six months later and found 700,000 in the same area! By taking up space, mussels have decimated the eighteen native clam species of Lake St. Clair, which lies between Michigan and Ontario. These mussels also filter the phytoplankton out of a huge volume of water, as much as a quart a day per mussel. Biologists are concerned that by eating so much phytoplankton, the mussels will leave less food for other species.

At the moment, biologists are working on ways to stop the spread of the zebra mussel. But their predictions are not promising. Zebra mussels are spreading, traveling by boat, by stream water, by floodwater, by bait bucket, and perhaps even stuck on duck feet, to other bodies of water. Billions of dollars will likely be spent in the next decade battling the effects of this tiny mollusk.

fish species such as trout, bass, and salmon. Some species are introduced when pet owners and sellers dump exotic fish from aquariums into lakes or when fishermen dump leftover bait fish—which are often nonnative—into ponds and lakes. People build channels to connect lakes and streams, and organisms swim through these channels, spreading far and wide. Organisms are also transported inside ships, in ballast water. This is water that ships pump in and out to balance their cargo during loading, unloading, and transport.

New Solutions   To combat the exotic species problem, a new federal law was passed in 1990 and strengthened in 1993. Called the Nonindigenous Aquatic Nuisance Prevention and Control Act, it requires freighters to exchange their freshwater ballast, mid-ocean, for saltwater ballast instead. The salt water is likely to kill the freshwater organisms picked up in European lakes and rivers. And the creatures in the saltwater ballast would be likely to die when they reached the fresh water of the Great Lakes. It's not a perfect solution, but scientists hope it will slow the invasion of exotic species by at least one route.

TOO MUCH OF A GOOD THING

A group of Native Americans named themselves Winnebago, meaning "stinking water," for the water they lived beside. Years later, French explorers called the place "Baye des Puants"—"Bay of Stinkers." Today, it's simply called Green Bay. This shallow extension of Lake Michigan is green because its waters are nutrient-rich and its algae grow thick. And it stinks because decaying plant matter naturally makes the water smell.

Growth Spurts   Green Bay gets its nutrient wealth from rainwater and river water that pick up minerals from rock and soil. Lakes can also get their nutrients from decaying organic animals and plants. Animals' droppings, their left-overs, and dead organisms sink down in lakes. These valuable mineral sources can stay locked up in the lake bottom, because the water stratifies, forming layers that prevent mixing. During spring and fall, however, these layers disappear and wind stirs the water. So nutrients and oxygen are well distributed, and plants and animals undergo a spurt of growth.

Attack of the Killer Algae   Why is Green Bay so green? Because, like other plants, when algae are fertilized by a lot of nutrients, they grow much thicker and spread. The population explodes, creating an algal bloom, a thick growth of algae that covers the water's surface. When this occurs, the lake begins undergoing a process of change called eutrophication. The blanket of algae blocks light. So plants below, sunlight-deprived, die. The bacteria that break down dead plants, and dead algae, use up the water's oxygen. Fish and other creatures suffocate. Their bodies wash ashore. These decay as well.

Who's to Blame   Sometimes lake waters, such as those in Green Bay, are naturally eutrophic—nutrient-rich and full of algae and decaying plant matter. But people's activities can also make clear, clean waters into green, eutrophic ones. This occurs when people pollute lakes and ponds with too many nutrients. Sources include manure, human sewage, phosphates in detergents, fertilizers that wash off farm fields and lawns, and nitrates released by industry. These materials overload lakes with nutrients, causing them to become more eutrophic over time.

THE LIFE AND DEATH OF PONDS AND LAKES

Lakes are not permanent features of the landscape. Once they form, they start dying right away. They fill in with sediment from rivers and runoff, and the remains of dead animals and plants. Eventually, a lake becomes a plant-filled lake, then a wetland, and eventually dry land. This process of transformation is a kind of succession, as when an abandoned farm field fills in with trees to become a forest.

The Tightening Noose   Succession occurs in a fairly orderly sequence. As the lake fills with sediment and decaying plants, plants near shore move inward, toward the center of the lake. They send out roots and shoots to colonize the newly created shallows. Reeds and cattails "march" out, and then shrubs such as buttonbush, and willow and alder trees follow. The open-water portion of the lake shrinks as the shore plants grow inward and the lake fills.

How Fast?   How fast the lake fills depends on many factors, including the amount and kind of sediment flowing into it. The growth and death rates of plants and animals also affect the process, determining how fast dead matter piles up. Succession can happen to a small pond in a century, or to a lake in a few thousand years. Whether natural or human-caused, eutrophication causes a massive die-off of plants and animals. These decaying organisms can help fill in a lake and accelerate its conversion to dry land. Overall, in the landscape, most lakes and ponds are ephemeral features—never permanent anyway. But people can influence how long lakes and ponds survive, and their ecological health and usefulness.

⚡ 7 ⚡
SALT LAKES
AND SODA LAKES

Even if you can't float in a swimming pool, you'll float if you jump into the Dead Sea. The Dead Sea is so salty that it's hard to dive down in it. Salt increases the water's density, buoying you up. You can hardly sink or swim, even by trying. All you can do is float. This is just one of many features that make salt and soda lakes so fascinating.

SALT AND SODA LAKE BASICS

Even water in a freshwater lake isn't pure; it contains a variety of salts and minerals. But to qualify as a salt or soda lake, a lake's water must contain more than 0.1 ounce per quart (3 grams per liter) of salt or soda. Seawater is much saltier than this lower limit, with about 1.3 ounces per quart (35 grams per liter) of salt. On the other hand, the Dead Sea, the saltiest lake on earth, is ten times saltier than ocean water!

Not Just Table Salt If you're floating in the Dead Sea, don't swallow the water. Reportedly, it tastes horrible because it contains chemical salts, other than the "salt shaker" kind. Some lakes, such as the Great Salt Lake, do contain mostly table salt—sodium chloride. But the Dead Sea and other lakes contain salts of other kinds, including mag-

*Utah's Great Salt Lake contains large amounts of table salt —
sodium chloride. Salt is visible, dried out, along the shore.*

nesium. Soda lakes contain carbonates, chemicals that often
bubble from hot, volcanic springs.

More Salt, Please . . .   Where do lakes get all those salts
and carbonates? From water, which picks up salts and carbonates from rocks over which it flows. Springs, rivers, and
runoff bring these chemicals into lakes, making them salty.
Over time, lakes can become much, much saltier. That's
because when water evaporates from a lake's surface, it
does not take dissolved chemicals along. The water evaporates, and the salts and carbonates become more and more
concentrated in the remaining lake water. The Great Salt
Lake, for instance, is only the dried-up remnant of a much
larger lake, Lake Bonneville. If water entirely disappears
from a salt lake, pond, or puddle, it may leave behind a
basin of white, glistening salt called a salt pan.

Former Seas A few salt lakes, such as the Caspian Sea, started out differently. They began as part of the sea, and over time were cut off from the sea by geological processes, thereby forming a lake. Ironically, the Caspian Sea, which has the largest surface area of any lake in the world, is actually becoming dilute—less salty—over time. That's because Volga River water now pouring into it is diluting the lake's waters.

Where in the World? Salt and soda lakes tend to be shallow, and more common in climates that are warm, where evaporation is rapid. These lakes are found in the western United States, Central Asia, East Africa, and Australia. But they can also form in Antarctica and at high altitudes.

Salt Harvest Much of the salt you buy in the store comes not from salt lakes but from mined underground salt deposits. Table salt and salts of other kinds are only occasionally mined from salt lakes. Potash—for fertilizer—is mined from the Dead Sea today. One way people mine chemicals from these lakes is by walling off part of the lake, letting that portion dry out, and gathering up the remaining salt. People traditionally gathered salts from the shores of salt lakes, because salt forms on the water's surface and winds push the salty crust ashore.

SALT LOVERS AND OTHERS

Sea monkeys, which you can buy in packets from your local pet store, are neither monkeys nor from the sea. But just add water to the powder in these packets, and you will have tiny pets, overnight. These creatures are actually brine shrimp, harvested from the Great Salt Lake and other lakes. They're just one of the unusual creatures that thrive in and near salt and soda lakes.

Why Salt Matters Brine shrimp have a tough skin that keeps most water and salt out of their body. That's necessary, because balancing the amount of salt in an animal's body is critical to its survival. A simple animal cell, if it's put in water that's too salty, will collapse and shrivel, because the water inside flows out. A simple cell put in water that's too dilute (not salty enough) will rupture. Water from outside the cell rushes in and fills it too full, which causes it to explode. That's why animals' bodies must be adapted to avoid these stresses on their cells. Most live only in water of a particular salinity. When they're put in the wrong salinity, they die.

Salt Lovers Plants and animals that are adapted to live in salty environments are termed halophilic, from the words *halo*, meaning "salt," and *philic*, meaning "loving." Creatures such as flies, worms, fish, and shrimp live in salt lakes around the world. But only a handful of microorgan-

*A tiny brine shrimp has been magnified
many times in this close-up view.*

isms can survive in the saltiest of waters: the waters of the Dead Sea. One salt-loving bacterium is so specifically adapted to the Dead Sea that it disintegrates if put in less salty water, such as ocean water. The bacterium, *Halobacterium halobium,* has a strange purple pigment that lets it trap the sun's energy. Some scientists have been investigating whether this bacterium could lead industry to a new way of making electricity.

Disaster-proof Eggs   Sea monkeys—brine shrimp—produce two kinds of eggs: thin-skinned ones that hatch quickly, and hard-shelled ones that enter a resting stage called diapause. Eggs in diapause must be dehydrated, then rehydrated before they hatch. They're hardy to the extreme. You

---

• THE INCREDIBLE SHRINKING LAKE •

Lakes, like any aquatic biome, need clean water, and plenty of it. Mono Lake in California is shrinking, its wildlife dying, because water from the streams that feed it is being used up by the city of Los Angeles. Sixty percent of Mono Lake's water has been cut off. The lake's salinity has doubled, its water level has dropped by 45 feet (13.7 meters), and its area has decreased by almost one-third. The change in the lake's water level is proving disastrous for many of the hundreds of thousands of gulls, phalaropes, ducks, and grebes that nest at the lake or feed there during migration. According to biologists, the shrimp and flies that these birds depend upon will not survive the salinity increase that will occur in the next few decades, as the lake's water level continues to fall. For Mono Lake, water scarcity is the major threat to its survival. For most lakes, however, water pollution is more of a concern.

can bake them at 212°F (100°C), freeze them to -310°F (-190°C), and add water, and they'll still hatch. This adaptation is important for a creature that could be dried out or exposed as lake water levels change. This ability also makes it possible for the eggs stored on a pet store shelf to remain viable. Often sold as fish food, these tiny creatures are a quick, defenseless meal for fish. And why not? In their natural habitats, the Great Salt Lake or California's Mono Lake, there aren't any fish to bother them.

Super-strainers Pink flamingo ornaments are found on people's lawns. But the wild ones belong in soda lakes. These long-legged birds reach down with their long necks and shuffle their upside-down bills side to side. A built-in sieve filters food from the water, working much like the baleen of a whale.

Flamingos use their bills to strain food from lake water.

SPECTACULAR ABUNDANCE

Very few species of animals actually live in the waters of salt and soda lakes. But the organisms that do live in these habitats often occur in great numbers. Mineral-rich waters allow microscopic plants, and the tiny animals that eat them, to flourish. On the shore of Mono Lake, someone once counted 4,000 brine flies perching on a single square foot of land. (Native Americans once scooped up the fly larvae to make food.) Mono Lake has so many brine shrimp that 250 tons are harvested a year.

Ducks and wading birds benefit from the abundance of flies, worms, copepods, and other small food in salt and soda lakes. Mono Lake plays host to hundreds of thousands of birds, which feed on its abundant flies and shrimp. Africa's soda lakes are so crawling with life they can serve up a sun-warmed meal of copepods to more than a million flamingos a day. These lakes are particularly important to birds' survival because they're often the only food and watering places in hundreds and thousands of miles of desert and semidesert.

❧ 8 ❧
PEOPLE AND
LAKES AND PONDS

People expect a lot from lakes and ponds. They expect clean drinking water and abundant fish to catch. They expect a place to swim, to sail, and to relax. At the same time, they also want water for use in industrial and power plants, and a place to dump the wastewater when they are done. All these activities call on the same biome: lakes and ponds.

THE CLEAN-WATER BLUES

Birds with twisted beaks. Fish with cancer. Ailing beluga whales. In the Great Lakes, and waters flowing into and out of them, the effect of toxic substances is tragically obvious. Toxic substances are poisons, chemicals that can be hazardous even in small amounts. Some cause cancer, birth defects, liver damage, nervous system disorders, or even death. DDT, PCBs, dioxin, and mercury are among the main group causing concern. These chemicals are produced as pesticides, as by-products of industrial processes, and during the burning of waste. The Great Lakes' basin, a hub of industry and agriculture, is particularly polluted, with 362 toxic chemicals in its waters.

Dilute or Deluded?   Industry claims that when pollutants are pumped into water, they're so greatly diluted they aren't a significant health risk. But the health risks of these chemicals at small concentrations, and in combination with each other, are not well understood. And these toxins also become concentrated once again as they pass through the natural food web.

Playing the Numbers   Fish-eating top predators, such as beluga whales, gulls, cormorants, eagles, and people, are the most at risk from toxic chemicals in the environment. That's because PCBs, DDT, chlordane, mirex, and many other chemicals build up in an animal's body fat, over time. And it also takes many plankton to feed a small fish, and many of those small fish to feed a bigger fish, and many of those bigger fish to feed a herring gull. At each step of the energy pyramid, toxic chemicals become concentrated, in a process called biomagnification. A herring gull, for instance, will have PCB levels in its body at least *thirty-three million times* greater than the amount of PCB in the water. Unfortunately, like fish-eating birds such as herring gulls, fish-eating people build up extremely high PCB levels, too. That's why state agencies and local health authorities sometimes issue warnings telling people not to eat fish from lakes, especially particular regions of the Great Lakes. So if you fish and eat your catch, it's wise to check with your local fish and game officials and environmental groups to see whether any warnings have been issued about lakes in your area.

What Goes Around . . .   For a long time, environmental efforts to battle lake pollution focused primarily on what was being dumped into the water. But more and more, people are realizing that what's in the air affects water quality, too. Rain and snow wash air pollutants into lakes, and some pollutants settle directly out of the air into lake water. Ninety percent of the PCBs in Lake Superior came from air

People may be harming gulls like this one by polluting the water where these birds find food.

pollution. Air pollutants from sources as far away as Central America are now being found in the Great Lakes.

Rain That Kills   Acid rain is one of the chief air pollutants damaging lakes. When pollutants emitted by automobiles, power plants, and industry are released into the air, they combine with water to form acids. These acids fall as rain, snow, sleet, and dry particles on lakes and ponds, acidifying them. And this acidity kills lake dwellers. Highly acidic water reacts chemically with rocks and soil, releasing naturally occurring aluminum from them. This aluminum washes into lakes. Aluminum can poison fish by making their gills inoperable. Acidity also interferes with fish's nervous systems, weakens fish's bones, and can kill snails, worms, and aquatic insects they depend upon.

Damaged Lakes   In Sweden, 4,000 lakes are now so acidified that fish cannot survive in them. And in the eastern United States, thousands of lakes have become so acidified their fish populations are threatened. How badly acid rain damages a lake or pond depends on the geology of the lake basin and the surrounding land. Lakes on certain kinds of rock can neutralize small amounts of acid rain, although eventually they, too, can be damaged by the pollution. Sweden is spending $25 million to add lime to 3,000 of its lakes, in order to neutralize their acidity, at least for the short term.

Globe-trotting Pollution   Air pollution is a global problem, one that crosses national boundaries. Much of the pollution that plagues Scandinavia wafts over from industries in Eastern Europe. Factories in the United States' Midwest and Northeast emit air pollution that damages Canadian lakes. That's why new global treaties and national laws that limit air pollution are the best hope for preserving healthy lakes and ponds.

MAKE A MINI-POND FOR WILDLIFE

You can create a small pool or pond that will attract wildlife to your backyard or school yard. Such a pool can provide a drink for a squirrel, a place for birds to bathe, a site where frogs can lay their eggs, and a habitat for interesting aquatic creatures you can study.

To carry out this project, you'll need the cooperation of your parents or guardians and the owners of the property where you plan to build. You should also check with local government about any regulations dealing with fencing off pools or ponds.

Using the books listed at the end of this activity, do some extra research on pond building before you begin. You'll need to research and experiment on your own to make the pond you build just right for your area.

First, measure the area you have to work with. Then create a water-holding basin for your pond. If your soil has a lot of clay, it may hold water without a liner. (Dig a small hole in the ground and fill it with water to see if it drains away overnight.) If your soil does not hold water, then you'll need to line your pond. You can use any of the following, which are available at hardware stores and garden stores:

- A wooden barrel, cut in half (once the wood is wet, it shouldn't leak)
- A kids' fiberglass pool
- A premade pond liner
- Plastic sheeting made of PVC (polyvinyl chloride) or butyl rubber

Once you've decided on the liner, you can design your pool and dig an appropriate-sized hole for it. A pond need only be 5 to 6 inches (13 to 15 centimeters) deep to serve as a drinking place for wildlife. A deeper pond, 1 to 2 feet (30 to 60 centimeters) deep, can support fish and frogs.

Here are several things to keep in mind when you design your pool:

- A pool with shallows and depths can accommodate different kinds of animals. Mounds of rocks, logs, and other material can provide a perch for birds.
- To make the pond more natural-looking, cover the bottom with rock or sand. Blend in the sides of the plastic liner with soil and put in plants to cover the edges. Make sure the edge of the pond is accessible to animals, and that it's not too slippery. Be sure the pond is not difficult for animals to reach when they want a drink.
- Carefully choose a water source for your pond. Water can evaporate quickly from a pond in summer, so you need to be willing and able to replenish

it easily. You can pipe in water that runs off your roof through a downspout. You can carry water to it yourself.

- A shady pond will remain cool and lose water less quickly in summer. In winter, you may need to purchase a birdbath heater to keep the pool from freezing.
- A drip hose or a recirculating pump will keep the water active, which attracts birds and discourages mosquitoes. (Frogs and fish take care of mosquitoes, too.)

Once you've built the pond, let the water sit for a while so the chemicals in it will settle out. Watch and see what animals in your area are attracted to your pond. Later, you may want to stock your pond with fish or frogs. Once you've tried working with this kind of small pond, you may want to move on to making a larger pond that could support large fish and birds. For information on landscaping for wildlife, consult:

Backyard Wildlife Habitat Program
National Wildlife Federation
1412 Sixteenth Street, NW
Washington, DC 20036-2266

(They have a program that certifies backyards and school yards as official wildlife habitats.)

Book list:
Garden Pools and Fountains by the editorial staff of Ortho Books (Ortho Books, 1988).
Pools, Ponds, and Waterways by Dan Tucker Grinstain (Grove/Atlantic Monthly Press, 1992).
Water Gardens by Peter Spadelmann (Barron's, 1992).

LAKE ERIE: BROUGHT BACK FROM THE DEAD

In the 1960s, journalists pronounced Lake Erie dead. It had been showing signs of dying for a while: beaches closing because of polluted waters, mayfly larvae disappearing from the lake bottom, dead fish washing ashore. By the 1960s, algae bloomed on the lake surface, in slimy, stinking green mats 2 feet (61 centimeters) thick. The Cuyahoga River, which flowed into Lake Erie, was so polluted with tires, wood, and oil that it caught fire in 1969!

The other Great Lakes were showing signs of pollution, too. But Erie, especially shallow and nutrient-rich, was particularly vulnerable to pollution. And billions of gallons of water polluted with human waste, fertilizers, pesticides, and industrial waste were being dumped into the lake every day. The fisheries were declining, the drinking water

This photograph shows Lake Erie's shoreline at its worst, polluted by solid waste and masses of algae.

smelled bad, and the water, in places, was too filthy to swim in. Something had to be done.

"Save Lake Erie!" came the public outcry. Working together, people from Canada and the United States pressured national, state, and local governments to pass laws to prevent pollution from flowing into the lake. The U.S. Clean Water Act of 1972, the International Great Lakes Water Quality Agreement, and various other items of legislation helped get the job done. Much of the chemical dumping was stopped. Phosphates in household detergents were reduced. By getting rid of these phosphates, and treating sewage before its release, people stopped "feeding" the great masses of algae. Fisheries' biologists reintroduced predatory fish, which had declined, into the lake. This helped balance the small, exotic fish that were multiplying. Billions of dollars were spent to clean up Lake Erie.

Today, these efforts have paid off. Erie has come back from the dead. The amount of algae has decreased. The huge algal blooms are gone, and the water doesn't stink in most places anymore. The levels of PCBs have decreased in some lake fishes. And the walleye population has rebounded and is doing quite well. People can once again swim and fish in parts of the lake.

In this case, people working together achieved an environmental victory, a cleanup that many people did not even believe was possible. Now that much of the visible pollution is being taken care of, new environmental challenges loom. Chief among these challenges are toxic chemicals and exotic species.

Heartened by past successes, people all around Lake Erie and the other Great Lakes are working hard to protect the health of these lakes. In March 1995, the United States Environmental Protection Agency revealed a new plan, called the Great Lakes Initiative, which is designed to

Taking samples is the first step in monitoring
water pollution in lakes and ponds.

reduce twenty-two of the most dangerous chemicals polluting the lakes. With government efforts that limit industrial
pollution, and citizen activists monitoring pollution, the
lake's future looks very positive.

MORE CLEANUP AND PRESERVATION EFFORTS

People all over the world are working to protect the health
of lakes and the wildlife that live in lakes. Here are some
specific efforts:

• In Nashville, Tennessee, second graders did extra chores
  at home to raise money to build a nesting island for loons.
  In Montana, kids posted signs to protect a loon nesting
  lake. And in Washington State, kids held a "Loonsday"
  walk to raise funds for loon conservation.
• With the help of the National Wildlife Federation's

Campus Ecology Program, students at Northland College in Ashland, Wisconsin, are making their college into a model campus, trying to reduce their discharge of pollutants into Lake Superior to zero.

- On Walpole Island, Ontario, high-school students and adults of the northern Ottawa, Potawatomi, and Ojibwa tribes are studying and noting changes in the abundance of zebra mussels, an exotic species that threatens Lake St. Clair. Students are also monitoring water pollution and reporting releases of untreated pollution to local authorities.
- On the southern shore of Lake Baikal, Russian elementary- and secondary-school students are monitoring the pollution content of the water almost daily. They are also networking with students worldwide by computer, to share information on lake problems and solutions.
- In Africa, Kenyan students are monitoring pollution in rivers that discharge into Lake Nakuru, a soda lake where millions of flamingos feed. They're also working with local community officials to reduce that pollution.
- Through a global network called GREEN (Global Rivers Environmental Education Network) elementary-, middle-, and high-school students in North America, Latin America, Asia, Africa, and Europe are monitoring water quality and exchanging information, by letter and computer, about their local rivers and lakes.

Global efforts to save lakes and ponds are in full swing, and students are a big part of the movement. In some cases, their efforts involve reducing pollution—air pollution such as acid rain and water pollution of all kinds—at its source. In other cases, they are working to preserve lakeshores and aid wildlife populations. And some people are creating lakes and ponds to provide wildlife habitat. With so many concerned people working to preserve them, lakes and ponds of the future could very well be in better shape than they are today. But there's still a need for more helping hands. To find out how *you* can get involved in these efforts, read the next section.

RESOURCES AND WHAT
YOU CAN DO TO HELP

Here's what you can do to help ensure that lakes and ponds are conserved:

• Learn more by reading books and watching videos and television programs about lakes and ponds. Check your local library, bookstore, and video store for resources. Here are just a few of the books available for further reading:

At the Water's Edge: Nature Study in Lakes, Streams, and Ponds by Alan B. Cvancara (John Wiley, 1989).
The Audubon Society Nature Guide to Wetlands by William A. Niering (Alfred A. Knopf, 1985).
Fish: An Enthusiast's Guide by Peter B. Moyle (University of California Press, 1993).
Fish Watching by C. Lavett Smith (Comstock, 1994).
The Late, Great Lakes: An Environmental History by William Ashworth (Wayne State University Press, 1987).
The Natural History of Lakes by Mary J. Burgis (Cambridge University Press, 1987).
Ponds and Pond Life by Anita Ganeri (Franklin Watts, 1993).

• For more information on conservation issues related to lakes and ponds, contact the following organizations:

Freshwater Foundation
2500 Shadywood Road
Navaire, MN 55331
Phone 1-612-471-9773

North American Loon Fund
6 Lily Pond Road
Gilford, NH 03246
Phone 1-603-528-4711
or their Canadian affiliate:

Canadian Lakes Loon Survey
Long Point Bird Observatory
P.O. Box 160
Port Rowan, ON N0E 1M0

If you like the job these organizations are doing, consider becoming a member.

• Improve lake and pond habitat by building nest boxes for wood ducks, constructing nesting platforms for loons, helping clean up lakeshores, and other activities. For information, contact your local soil conservation service office or state fish and game department. Naturalists at local parks with lakes and ponds may also know who's doing projects in your area. You can also contact the North American Loon Fund or the Canadian Lakes Loon Survey for information on these activities.

• Get your class, ecology club, 4-H Club, Girl Scout troop, Boy Scout troop, or other organization involved in monitoring and preventing pollution in a stream or river near you. Stream water runs into lakes. Have your teacher, leader, or adviser contact the following organization for information:

Global Rivers Environmental Education Network (GREEN)
721 East Huron Street
Ann Arbor, MI 48104
Phone 1-313-761-8142
Internet: green@green.org

• Get your class involved in activities related to lakes. Have your teacher contact one of the following organizations:

International Joint Commission
Great Lakes Regional Office
P.O. Box 32869
Detroit, MI 48232-2869
Phone 1-313-226-2170
or the same organization in Canada at:

100 Ouellette Ave., 8th floor
Windsor, ON N9A 6T3
Phone 1-519-257-6735
(Ask for their *Directory of Great Lakes Educational Material.*)

National Project Wet
Culbertson Hall
Montana State University
Bozeman, MT 59717
Phone 1-406-994-5392
(This organization publishes a variety of water-related educational guides and can connect educators with Project Wet activities and coordinators in their state.)

North American Lake Management Society
P.O. Box 5443
Madison, WI 53705-5443
Phone 1-608-233-2836
(Ask for their *Environmental Education Resources Directory.*)

- Use chlorine-free, unbleached recycled paper. Chlorine used in bleaching paper to make it white becomes dioxin later in the manufacturing process. Dioxin is a potent carcinogen—a cancer-causing chemical. Paper mills are major contributors of toxic waste to the Great Lakes. For a catalog of environmental products, including unbleached paper, contact:

Earth Care Paper
Ukiah, CA 95482-8507
Phone 1-800-347-0070

Seventh Generation
Colchester, VT 05446-1672
Phone 1-800-456-1177

- Reduce your use of batteries and use rechargeable batteries whenever possible. Batteries contain mercury. When batteries are incinerated, as they are in many solid-waste disposal facilities, the mercury is spread in the air and can get into lakes. Mercury is highly toxic, deadly to humans and wildlife. Look for rechargeable batteries in local stores. Or you can get them through Real Goods, which also sells other energy-saving products. For a catalog, write or call:

Real Goods
966 Mazzoni Street
Ukiah, CA 95482-3471
Phone 1-800-762-7325

- Find out where your water comes from. Then work to reduce your water use. The less water you use, the more water is available for aquatic animals and plants. Try taking shorter, more efficient showers, and using less water when brushing your teeth. Your family might be able to install more efficient shower heads, faucets, and low-flow toilets. Reduce the amount of water used on lawns by watering in the evening, when less water evaporates. Better yet, plant other kinds of plants that are native to your area and don't require as much water as a lawn does. For information on water-saving devices, see the catalogs above.

• Write letters to state and national government officials, telling them you feel lake and pond conservation is important.

GLOSSARY

aquatic   of water, having to do with water, or living in water

biomagnification   the process by which toxic chemicals accumulate in animals' body tissues and are passed through the food web in such a way that top predators accumulate the greatest concentration of toxic chemicals

biome   an area that has a certain kind of community of plants and animals. In the case of terrestrial biomes, but not aquatic biomes, they have a certain climate as well.

diapause   a dormant period when an organism's body functions slow or cease, in order to survive difficult conditions

epilimnion the warm, top layer of a lake in summer

euphotic zone   the light-filled layer near the lake's surface, where 99 percent of sunlight penetrates

eutrophication   the process by which a lake becomes rich in nutrients, which spurs abundant algae growth. This leads to the eventual die-off of the algae, and their decomposition by bacteria. The bacterial decomposition uses up so much of the water's oxygen that fish and other aquatic organisms may suffocate.

halophilic   describes an organism that is adapted to live in salt water. Halophilic literally means "salt loving."

hypolimnion   the lower level of a lake that has stratified because of temperature and density; the lake region below the thermocline

lake-effect   influenced by proximity to lakes. Usually refers to weather phenomena, such as clouds, breezes, snowfalls, fogs, and storms.

limnologist   a scientist who studies lakes

macrophytes   aquatic plants that are macroscopic, meaning they are big enough to see without a microscope

paleolimnologist   a scientist who studies fossilized material found in lakes

predator   an animal that hunts, kills, and consumes other animals

phytoplankton   tiny—microscopic or slightly larger—aquatic plants that float in water

profundal zone   the lower layer of a lake, reached by less than 1 percent of sunlight. Plants cannot survive in this zone. The depth at which it occurs depends on the clarity of the water.

salt lake   a lake containing a high concentration of salts. Table salt (sodium chloride) is one of many kinds of salts.

salt pan   a basin, often found in deserts, where water evaporates, leaving a mineral crust of salt behind

sediment   particles of material that are transported and deposited by water, wind, or ice

seiche   a slow wave that forms as water sloshes back and forth in a lake basin. Seiches are caused by earthquakes or by strong winds piling up water on one end of a lake.

soda lake   an alkaline lake containing large amounts of carbonates

stratification   the formation of layers

succession   the replacement of one ecological community by another as environmental conditions change

thermocline   a layer of lake water, located between the epilimnion and hypolimnion, where water temperature decreases quickly and density increases quickly with depth

water cycle   the endless, global circulation of water through aquatic biomes, terrestrial biomes, and the atmosphere. The heating power of the sun drives the cycle, by causing evaporation. The water cycle is also called the hydrologic cycle.

zooplankton   tiny—microscopic or slightly larger—floating animals

INDEX

paleolimnologists, 24, 25
PCBs, 56, 57, 63
phytoplankton, 11, 26, 28, 30,
    41–43, 45
pink flamingos, 5, 54, *54*, 55, 65
plankton, 57
pollen, 24, 28
pollutants, 56–58, 65
pollution, 57–59, 62–65
    monitoring, *64*
pond scum, 34
power plants, 56, 58
profundal zone, 10

re-formed rivers, 22
reservoirs, 13
rivers, 5, 6, 9, 15, 17, 23, 45, 46,
    51, 62

salt harvest, 51
salt pan, 50
schistosomiasis, 32
sea lamprey, 43, *43*
sea monkeys, 51, 53
sediment, 7, 10, 24, *24*, 47, 48
seeds, 28, 29, 36–37
seiches, 17
Sierra Nevada, *23*
sinkhole lakes, 21
slime layer, 29
sponges, 8, 38

St. Lawrence River, *14*, 15
still-water habitats, 7, 28
Superior, Lake, 13, 15, 18,
    57–58, 65
swimmer's itch, 32

Tahoe, Lake, 22
Tanganyika, Lake, 9
toxic substances, 56

volcano, 12, 21

wastewater, 56
water
    density, 10
    scarcity, 53
    sources, 16, 17
water cycle, 5, 6
water flow, 10
water level, 53
water molecule, 37
water pollution. *See* pollution.
waves, 5, 8, 15, 17, 18
Weir, Lake, 22
wetlands, 5, 24
Winnipeg, Lake, 12
wood frogs, 38, *38*

zebra mussels, 44, *44*, 45, 65
zooplankton, 10, 30, 33, 34

PHOTO CREDITS

To Bridget,

who knows how complicated and wonderful families can be.

SIMON & SCHUSTER BOOKS FOR YOUNG READERS
An imprint of Simon & Schuster Children's Publishing Division
1230 Avenue of the Americas, New York, New York 10020

Copyright © 2006 by Marissa Moss

A Paula Wiseman Book

SIMON & SCHUSTER BOOKS FOR YOUNG READERS
IS A TRADEMARK OF SIMON & SCHUSTER, INC.

Amelia® and the notebook design are
registered trademarks of Marissa Moss.

Book design by Amelia
(with help from Lucy Ruth Cummins)
The text for this book is hand-lettered.
Manufactured in the United States of America

2 4 6 8 10 9 7 5 3 1

CIP data for this book is available
from the Library of Congress.

ISBN-13: 978-0-689-87447-5   ISBN-10: 0-689-87447-2

We talked until I could see the moon rising outside her bedroom window. I told her about that last night in the hotel with Cleo, how great it was.

"Like it is with us now?" Carly asked. "When we tell each other everything?"

"Yeah," I said. "Just like now."

Neither of us said anything for a while. I was feeling how lucky I was with all my families — Cleo and Mom, Dad, Clara, and George, and here with Carly, my family of friends.

Finally Carly broke the silence. "Good night, Amelia."

"Good night," I whispered back.

And it was.

I smiled — that's how families are. But even the worst people have something good about them — like Cleo (though I still couldn't figure out what it was in Uncle Harold's case).

Carly couldn't wait to hear what happened.

She invited me to spend the night so we could talk all we wanted. I couldn't wait to tell her!

I brought her back a   souvenir from Texas — the cowboy hat. She loved it!

I was feeling so good about Cleo, I didn't even mind the flight home with her, but by the next day we were back to normal, fighting with each other like we always do. Mom was happy to have us back home — she was so happy, she didn't seem mad about Justin even. She thought the whole thing was hilarious.

That'll give your father a taste of raising teenagers — teenage <u>girls</u>!

I wonder if he'll be so eager to have you visit now!

↑ Like she was sure nothing like that would ever happen while she's in charge. She might be in for as much of a surprise as Dad was.

And I got a postcard from Nadia! ↙

Dear Amelia,
  How did the family reunion go? I hope it was a lot of fun. I know how tricky those things can be. At the last one our family had, my aunt walked out in a huff after my uncle insulted her taste in books, and one of my cousins bit another cousin. It was more like going to the zoo than going to a party! luv, Nadia

Fairy Tale Coaches~ Cinderella
40¢

Amelia
564 N. Homerest
Oopa, Oregon
97881

yours till the sun beams!

Somehow when you talk to someone while you're in bed, in the dark, everything sounds more secret and important and dramatic. It's a great feeling.

You can barely see the other person so their voice takes on a huge presence. It's magical!

"Cleo!" I whispered. "Are you awake?"

"If I wasn't before, I would be now. What do you want?"

"Are you glad you came?" I asked.

"Of course! I got to see Justin, didn't I? I just hope I can go to Chicago again and Mom doesn't ground me for life."

"I guess I'm glad I came too," I said, suddenly feeling sure of it. "And I'm glad I came with you this time."

"You are?" Cleo sounded surprised.

"Yeah." I smiled in the dark. "I like the way you see things sometimes. You're the perpetual optimist while I'm the constant worrier."

We talked for a long time - about families and boys and kissing. And a lot about Dad. Now that I've met ALL his family, he felt more part of mine than ever. I might still be figuring out how I fit in with everyone else, but I KNEW I belonged with him, even if we didn't live together, even if he'd missed practically my whole childhood.

It was the perfect end to the longest, biggest, most-fights-ever family reunion.

Hey, Cleo!
Thank you, thank you!
Clara, sitting by herself, looking lonely
Justin, ignoring me
Cleo
Cleo, blowing kisses as the star of the show
The baby horse, scrambling to stand up
The games and races
Cleo and Justin, kissing
Dad, looking old and sad and completely confused

Should I have stayed home? I was glad I'd met my grandparents. It was good to get a sense of family history from Grandpa's stories. And now Dad's relatives weren't a mystery to me. I still wasn't sure whether I liked some of them or not, but they definitely weren't scary.

All these images flashed through my head.
↓

Chloe?

Adelia?

Uncle Harold, being rude

Grandpa, winking at me

Goat!

You're not what I expected.

George, all excited about the animals

Tara, staring at me

That night Dad gave us both a big lecture about cousins and boyfriends and kissing. It was awful — I didn't want to hear any of it and neither did Cleo. We just nodded and said "Yes, uh huh, we understand" until he left. YUCCH!

Once he was gone, I teased Cleo. "I don't think that's what Dad meant by a family reunion."

Cleo stuck out her tongue at me. "Ha, ha, very funny. The worst part is, he'll tell Mom."

I hadn't thought of that. "So?" I shrugged. "What can she do?"

"Never let me out of her sight again!" Cleo huffed. "They both have to leave me alone and let me grow up!"

I got the feeling that what Cleo wanted was a family un-union — at least from Mom and Dad.

I slept on the floor that night on a pile of blankets. It was better than the bed or the bathroom floor.

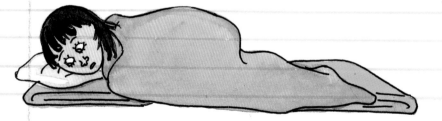

But I couldn't fall asleep. My head was too full of everything that had happened. Now that it was all over, I wondered if it was good I'd come or not.

Dad turned purple, Clara was bright pink, Marta was red, and her husband, Michael, was a sickly yellow. Cleo and Justin were surprised. Tara was triumphant.

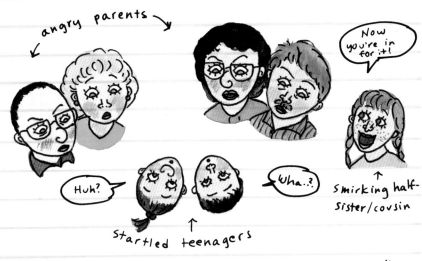

angry parents

Now you're in for it!

Huh?

Wha..?

Smirking half-sister/cousin

Startled teenagers

The rest of the reunion, all we heard were "kissing cousin" jokes (even though Justin isn't a _real_ cousin). We didn't stay long after that. Dad rushed us all back to the hotel. He was so mad, he didn't know what to say. I felt sorry for him. He's a great dad with George, but he's not used to older kids. Teenagers are beyond him. Especially one like Cleo.

I have to admit, I kind of admired her. She knew how to get what she wanted.

What's the big crime?

She sulked the whole drive back.

Or you can use the Cleo method — escape by spending the whole time with one other person. That method has its own risks, however, if you're not sure how you and the other person will get along for that much time. For Cleo and Justin, that wasn't an issue.

Tara was excited to give everyone the news.

Mom! Guess what I saw!

Come quick— to the barn!

You'll see!

I thought a cat had had a litter of kittens in the hay, something like that, but nooooooo, it wasn't that. It was Cleo and Justin, sitting in the barn, K - I - S - S - I - N - G !

⑥ Spend time at the drinks table. Mix up experiments, potions, whatever.

⑦ Spend time _under_ the drinks table.

⑧ If you're really bored, go out to the parking lot and try to match the people to their cars.

⑨ Make future plans that you have no intention of keeping.

⑩ Leave early.

③ Talk in a thick accent so it's hard for anyone to understand what you're saying.

*translation: "I love to read, don't you?"

④ Ask a lot of questions. People love to talk about themselves and that way you don't have to tell them anything about yourself.

⑤ Eat — no one expects you to talk with your mouth full.

It all made me realize I wasn't the only one who wasn't sure they belonged. There was no one right way to fit in — it seemed like everyone was finding their own place, even if that place was on the edge of things. Still, there had to be ways to make it easier.

HOW TO SURVIVE FAMILY GET-TOGETHERS
IN 10 EASY STEPS!

① Arrive late — traffic is always a good excuse, no matter what time of day it is, rush hour or not.

So sorry it took us so long to get here.

They were re-paving the road, which meant a total clog. And then that truck lost its load...

② Wear makeup that discourages people from getting too close.

This? On my cheeks? Yes, I'm seeing a doctor about it. No one can quite figure out what it is yet.

Don't worry — doubt i contagio

Harold's kids terrorized Marta's kids — especially Tyler. He was a total bully.

Tara told me some of these secrets but some I figured out on my own.

It's not true that Harold had a good side, like Grandpa said. Either side is yucchy. No one likes him because he's hypercompetitive, always showing off his latest toy (today it was a teeny, tiny digital camera), and he's plain old rude. Why does he say these things except to hurt people's feelings? Why does practically everything he says start with "I" or "my"?

Julie's husband, Jeff, is so quiet and shy, no one talks to him. I think he should get together with Clara. Then they'd both feel better. →

"What plans?" I asked after Harold finally walked away.

"NOT going to his house for brunch," Dad said. "ANYTHING but that!" He winked at me.

I laughed. And just that little thing made me love Dad more than ever. I felt like he was on my side and always would be.

The rest of the afternoon there were games like sack races, 3-legged races, bingo, charades, that kind of thing. It was actually fun because I didn't have to talk to anyone. And sometimes it was like being in a big soap opera. After spending several hours with Dad's family I realized there were all kinds of hidden stories and crazy relationships.

FAMILY SECRETS

The wives of Dad's brothers hated each other.
↓

She thinks she's so great!

What a snob!

Clara thought everyone hated her, but they didn't - they just weren't friendly.
↓

Why don't they like me?

What have I done?

Grandpa made a toast, thanking everyone for coming. He named the people who had traveled the farthest and who the new babies were. He didn't mention me and Cleo. I couldn't figure it out — was I part of this family or not?

Then Dad introduced me to his other brother, Jerome, and to his other sister, Julia. At least they got my name right and they didn't say anything mean about Mom. Harold came over too, trying to be all jokey and friendly. I wasn't sure about my other aunts and uncles, but I definitely didn't like _him_.

No hard feelings, eh, Amelia? I've always liked your mother — she's really something else. You have to understand, divorce is hard on everyone. It's never easy when there are kids involved.

If he said one more cliche, I swear I was going to scream. Lucky for him, he didn't. Instead he invited us over to his house the next day for a big post-reunion brunch. I groaned. That was the last thing I wanted — _more_ reunion after _this_ reunion. I just wanted to go home. I was so relieved when Dad said we had other plans.

"That's my girl." He turned to Cleo on the other side of the table. "How about you, Cleo? You haven't heard the family history either."

"Thanks, Grandpa," Cleo said, the word sliding like butter out of her mouth. Easy for her! Everything was easier for her! "But Justin and I are going on a hayride as soon as we finish lunch. Later, okay?"

I could tell Grandpa was disappointed, but he just nodded. "Go have fun," he said.

Cleo wiped her barbeque-saucy hands and leaped up. Justin followed her. It was enough to make me want to puke, but Marta thought they were "adorable." She said Justin had been looking forward to the reunion for weeks because of Cleo. I wished somebody had felt that way about me. Suddenly Cleo's fantasy of being the star of the show didn't seem so silly — she was certainly the star of Justin's show.

Cleo got an adoring fan and I got family stories. It didn't seem fair.

Cleo, blowing kisses at her doting public. →

SMACK!

SMACK!

Thank you, thank you, everyone! I love you all!

Cleo

Dad sat next to Clara and introduced me to his sister, Marta, her husband, Michael, and their daughter, Tina - Tara's sister. Tina stuck her tongue out at me.

Tara nudged me and hissed in my ear. "Okay, I fight with her, too, but you can see why, can't you?"

I nodded, waiting for the lump in my throat to go down, but it was lodged tight. I didn't think I could swallow anything. I felt so alone while Cleo looked completely comfortable, laughing with Justin and shoveling down food.

"Amelia, you're sitting next to me," Grandpa insisted. "We have a <u>lot</u> of catching up to do."

He winked at me and I felt better right away, just with that little wink. →

I know your dad hasn't told you any of the family stories — like how my parents came to America, what life was like before then...

Marta groaned. "Dad, don't bore her first thing. You'll scare her off this family and she'll never want to visit us again."

"No," I said, my voice suddenly unstuck, the lump gone. "I want to hear the stories. Please tell me." I waited. "Please, Grandpa?" There, I'd said it — Grandpa.

He beamed like he'd been waiting to hear those words.

"You're not what I expected, not how Cleo described you," she said. I rolled my eyes. "I bet. That's probably a good thing."

Before we could say anything else, Dad came up.

"There you are! I've been looking everywhere for you." He gave Tara a quick kiss, then told us it was time to eat. I wasn't sure whether I liked Tara or not, but I was definitely hungry and I wanted to eat with <u>someone</u> I knew, not just a bunch of strangers.

Everyone was streaming toward lines of tables that had been set up under awnings. I saw Cleo already sitting next to Justin and stuffing corn bread in her mouth. I noticed she hadn't saved a seat for me.

All I saw were unfamiliar faces until Grandpa waved and caught my eye. Grandma called us over, saying she'd saved us places. Clara looked relieved to see us and jumped up to take George. I realized I hadn't seen her talk to anyone. Maybe she felt as uncomfortable at this reunion as I did.

Tara wrinkled her nose. "I guess it's okay. We fight a lot. Dad says that's what brothers and sisters do, but I don't fight as much with my younger sister. I think it's because we have different moms, and Justin only lives with us half of the time, every other week. Plus, he hates my mom, so it's more peaceful when he's gone." She sighed. "At least my mom doesn't have kids from _her_ first marriage. My best friend has 3 half-siblings – one from her mom and two from her dad. It's a mess!"

And I thought _my_ family was complicated! I guess everyone feels that way.

"So my mom is your dad's sister. We see your family a lot since we all live in Chicago. But everyone else here..." Tara shrugged. "Some of them I see only once a year. And some I've never met before. Like you." She stared at me so intently I felt like something was wrong with my face.

Why are you looking at me like that?

Is something the matter?

I was pretty sure I looked okay.

No embarrassing stains or smudges. Maybe she didn't like my hat.

"You know how to ride?" The voice startled me. It came from a girl who was sitting on the fence next to George's stroller.

I walked up, shaking my head. "Not horses," I said. "Bikes, yes. I'm not from around here."

"Me neither," the girl said. "We live in Chicago. I'm Tara."

"I'm Amelia and this is my half-brother, George. He lives in Chicago too, with my dad and stepmother. Maybe you know them, Quentin and Clara?"

Tara's face split into a wide smile. "I know George and of course I know your dad and Aunt Clara. I've even met your sister. Cleo, right?"

I didn't know what to say. Everyone knew everyone else — except for me.

"I have a half-brother too," Tara added. "Only he's older, not cute and little. His name is Justin."

Finally! Someone I'd met, if only for a second.

"Oh, I know him! I mean, I just met him today. Is he nice? What's it like having an _older_ half-brother?"

Tara didn't look like Justin and she didn't have a jelly-roll nose → either.

she seemed nice — at least she was someone to ← talk to.

Then a big lump in the grass next to him moved. It was his mother, standing up. I was surprised because you never see horses lying down — they sleep standing up. Then I realized why the colt was having so much trouble with his legs — he must have just been born! That's why the mare had been lying down.

I climbed over the fence and walked slowly over to them. The mare looked at me and snorted, but she let me come close. I could see the foal was still wet from being inside of her. His hooves were soft and spongy and new, not yet hard. I held my breath, touching the colt gently. I felt like I'd been given a gift from the universe, to see someone so soon after they'd entered the world.

Then the mare ambled off and her baby followed. I stood there watching them, full of a strange, calm wonder. It was magical.

I was tempted to go back to the car and wait for the whole thing to be over. I wished I'd brought my notebook with me, but I'd left it at the hotel. Writing and drawing usually made me feel better. Now all I had to distract me was George and he'd fallen asleep. He was still cute, but not much fun that way.

I bumped the stroller over to the far back pastures and watched the horses. There were a couple of young colts, all knobby knees and gangly legs. I couldn't help it—watching them made me smile.

There was one especially small one who was so young, he had trouble organizing his legs. ↓

He kept on wobbling and falling, then unfolding his legs and trying again.

↑
Finally he got it right. He just stood there, looking really tired.

I looked at George. "Can this get any worse?" I asked. He didn't have an answer. Neither did I.

I got tired of sitting on the itchy hay bale and decided to take George exploring. →

What else was there to do? I didn't see Dad anywhere. My grandparents were surrounded by loving children and grandchildren. I didn't belong anywhere.

At least George was having a great time. We found the barn with the cows and a pen with sheep and goats. That was enough to thrill him. He was especially excited about the goats. I wished I was as little as him, back to the age when a smelly goat was my idea of fun, and I didn't care if people paid attention to me as long as I was fed and warm.

There were groups of kids running around, playing with each other, but I didn't know anyone and they all looked younger than me. I couldn't just barge in and join them.

The reality had to be a big disappointment. I actually felt sorry for her. That only lasted a minute, though, because some boy came up to us, and Cleo leaped to her feet, grinning, the prom queen once more.

Hey, Justin! How's it going?

Good. I've been looking all over for you. Wanna see the pond out back? It's kinda cool.

Sure, let's go!

Cleo turned to me. "Tell Dad I'm with Justin."
Justin looked at me like he'd just noticed my existence.
"Oh, is this your sister?" he asked.
"Yeah, that's Amelia." Cleo was already walking away.
And she'd complained about our grandparents not introducing us to anyone! She was way worse! She could have invited me to join them, but instead they were gone, leaving me alone with George. I should have just said I was coming too, I wanted to see the pond. Now I was abandoned.

"This sucks!" Cleo said. "Now they're afraid to talk to us or introduce us to anyone."

"Well, you weren't exactly polite," I pointed out.

"Neither was Harold — and he's a grown-up. He should know better." She slumped back in her chair. "I guess I was expecting everyone to be excited to see us after so long, like we would be the stars of the show. I thought the banner at the gate would say 'Welcome, Cleo and Amelia!' But no one cares that we bothered to come. Harold didn't even remember Dad talking about us!"

Wow. I hadn't imagined anything like that! While I was dreading how horrible this trip would be, Cleo was dreaming of some fantasy, lovey-dovey family reunion. I couldn't help it — I felt bad for her.

She had some kind of Miss America fantasy — like she would be on this big float, blowing kisses at her adoring fans.

I could tell that Cleo was still steamed. It would take a lot of ice to cool her down.

"You have to excuse Harold," Grandma said. (There — I called her Grandma, even if it's only in this notebook.) "He means well. He just doesn't always say the right thing."

"I'll say!" Cleo snapped. "He's a colossal jerk!"

"Come on," Grandpa urged. "He's also your uncle, so you need to see his good side. That's what families do — accept each other, the good _and_ the bad."

Cleo didn't say anything, but she looked at me and I could tell exactly what she was thinking — if this is what it means to have family around then no, thank you! I smiled at her because for once I felt exactly the same as she did.

We found the drinks, passing knots of people on the way who ran up and greeted Grandma and Grandpa or just waved and shouted hello. There were no more introductions and after Cleo and I were settled in a corner sipping sodas, they left us, saying they needed to find our aunts and uncles.

← I put some apple juice in George's sippy cup. The whole drama had passed right by him. Little kids are so lucky!

"Harold," Dad hissed through gritted teeth. "I told you the girls were coming. REMEMBER? This is their chance to meet all the family." He put one hand on Cleo's shoulder. "This is Cleo." He said her name **superslowly** and clearly like he was explaining a difficult foreign word. Then he put his other hand on my shoulder. "And this is Amelia. NOT Adelia. And you'll forgive me if I insist that you DON'T insult their mother."

"Oh, hey, sorry," Harold sputtered. "Guess I put my foot in my mouth with that one."

"There's no boot big enough to fill that hole!" Cleo sniped. I was impressed. Go, Cleo, I thought, you tell that jerk! But Dad gripped her shoulder tighter to calm her down.

"Now, now," Harold soothed. "No need to get nasty. We're all family here, aren't we? I said I was sorry, so let's shake and be friends."

Dad nodded. So we did. First Cleo, then me. Yucch! I wanted to wash my hand right away. Then Dad suggested our grandparents take us to get a drink while he and his brother chatted. We didn't need to be asked twice — we were all **eager** to escape.

I could tell Dad's feelings were hurt — after all, his parents WERE seeing how their grandkids had grown, just different ones than the bellowing man meant.

"Hello, Harold," Dad said. "I'd like to introduce you to my daughters."

Harold turned to us as if just noticing that we existed. He looked at us like he was examining a dent in his brand-new car.

"Chloe? Adelia?" His eyebrows pitched up like they were trying to escape his forehead. "Wow! I forgot you had daughters! What happened? Did that witch of an ex-wife finally let them out of her clutches? Halleluyah, miracles CAN happen!"

I was FURIOUS, but I didn't have to say anything because Dad was even madder than me.

His face was almost purple with rage. I thought he was going to yell, but his voice was calm and quiet and steely cold.

Harold looked totally surprised.

Whatever it was, I felt comfortable with them right away. I didn't even mind hugging them. I wanted to call them "Grandma" and "Grandpa," but somehow that was too much. The words stuck in my throat, so I didn't say anything. But I smiled. Maybe this reunion wouldn't be so bad after all.

I wanted to ask a million questions, like did they get along with Mom? Did they try to see us or did they give up like Dad had? Did they visit us a lot before the divorce? Did they approve of Dad marrying Mom in the first place? But I didn't get a chance to ask anything because a big man with a booming voice pushed in front of me to scoop up my grandmother in a bear hug.

I knew he had to be Dad's brother - he had the trademark jelly-roll nose. He looked like the uncle in my nightmare.

Mom! Dad! Come over and see how your grandkids have grown!

You won't recognize Tyler— he's taller than me now!

The first people we ran into were Dad's parents —
my grandparents. How ~~weird~~ ~~wierd~~ ~~weird~~ ~~wierd~~ weird!
For most of my life I didn't have any
grandparents. Now here they were.

It was even
stranger than the
spelling of this
annoying word!

There you
two are!
We've been
waiting for
this moment
for so long!

Such
grown-up young
ladies now!

The last time
we saw Amelia, she
was little enough to
fit inside a shoe
box!

My grandmother had
Cleo's nose! So that's
where it came from!
She had bluish hair
and bright orange
lipstick that made me
think of a troll doll.
But she wasn't a troll—
there was something
about her face that was
warm and kind.

My grandfather
had even less
hair on the top of
his head than Dad
did, but he had these strange
long wiry hairs growing out
of his eyebrows and ears.
He was really old and wrinkled,
but his eyes were bright blue
and sparkly and young.

I liked them both right away. Maybe deep down my
baby self remembered them — we had met before!

I put George in his stroller and felt safer being behind it, like he was a kind of shield. I have to admit, I was impressed by Cleo. She seemed totally fearless. Meeting so many strangers didn't faze her at all.

I can't wait for everyone to see how great I look.

I bet no one else has a pink cowboy hat and red boots. This is a real fashion statement.

Either she was incredibly brave or too full of herself to be worried. I wasn't sure which, but either way, I envied her. I wished I could be as calm as her — or like George, completely oblivious to what anyone thinks about him.

I adjusted my hat and tried to look like someone cool and interesting. →

← But what if there was no one cool and interesting for me to meet?

WELCOME TO THE SOLOKOVANSKY FAMILY REUNION

I thought Dallas was all big highways and tall, sleek buildings that look like giant cigarette lighters, but we drove past all the modern high-rises to a ranch that looked like something out of an old Western. There was a big gate with two L's linked together (for the Double L Ranch, according to Dad) and under it a bright blue banner with a welcome message. It was a strange mixture — the modern sign and all the festive balloons with the old-fashioned, weather-beaten gate.

Rows and rows of cars were parked outside — not a single horse at the hitching post. A lot of people were already there, and Dad said a lot more were coming. I got a sinking feeling in my stomach. Where did I fit in? I had no idea. It felt like the first day at a new school where you didn't even know which grade you belonged in — much less which class.

What a terrible dream! I was afraid to go back to sleep, so I got up and read my book in the bathroom. I seemed to be spending a lot of time in the bathroom these days and I didn't even have diarrhea.

This bathroom didn't have a sofa in it, just a cold tile floor with a small rug on it. This weekend was NOT a relaxing vacation, NOT a fun family visit. It was turning into the longest nightmare ever.

At breakfast Cleo said she'd slept great. Everyone had. Except me.

I could barely keep my eyes open. →

← I looked like I'd slept under a bed, not on one.

I decided to skip eating and went back to sleep for a couple of hours until Dad woke me up and said it was time to head for the ranch. I had such a bad case of bed head, I was grateful for the cowboy hat — no way I was EVER going to take it off.

I tried not to think about my bad dream and the possibility of it coming true. After all, Cleo doesn't know how to play the guitar. The whole thing was crazy! (Well, she doesn't know how to sing, but she still does.)

Even though her singing was screechy and off-key, everyone stamped their feet and clapped their hands. They loved her!

I had to get out of there, but a big man who looked like Dad but wasn't Dad — somehow in the dream I knew he was my uncle — grabbed me and shoved me to the front.

"Now, you behave!" he shouted. "Why can't you be more like your sister?"

"I don't want to be like her!" I yelled.

Suddenly everyone turned to look at me, their eyes red with anger and hatred.

"Get her!" someone shouted.

"Don't let her escape!" someone else screamed.

Hands reached for me from all sides. I panicked. I couldn't get away! I tried to yell for help!

And then I woke up.

I dreamed I was in a big corral crowded with people. Everyone was wearing cowboy outfits except me. I was still in my pajamas. I wanted to go home so I could get dressed, but I couldn't find the gate. All I could see were the backs of people with their hats. Everyone was looking at something in the center of the corral.

I squeezed through so I could see what was so interesting. Right in the middle of all those staring, smiling faces was Cleo! She was sitting on a tall stool, playing a guitar and singing.

That night was the worst night ever. Not because of what happened in the restaurant. Not because of what was going to happen the next day. Because of one big, fat reason—Cleo!

The sofa bed sagged in the middle, rolling Cleo and me together. No matter how much I tried to sleep on the edge of the bed, I couldn't.

me, staring at the ceiling, wide awake

rolled-up blanket

zzzzzzz z z z zzzzz

Cleo, sound asleep— nothing bothers her!

saggy, saggy mattress

If it weren't for the blanket I'd put between us, we would have been practically on top of each other. As it was, Cleo was way too close to me. I stuck wads of cotton in my ears and I could still hear her snoring. I kept on kicking and pushing at her until finally she rolled over and the snoring stopped. But I couldn't fall asleep. I felt like I was sliding down a cliff—the bed was so caved-in and lumpy. Sleeping on the floor would have been MUCH more comfortable.

I don't remember falling asleep but I must have, because the next thing I knew I had bolted wide-awake, sweating, from a HORRIBLE nightmare.

Would he send me back to Mom so I wouldn't ruin his big family event? Would he decide that one daughter was enough, he didn't need two? Would he tell me he'd made a terrible mistake answering my letter and he wanted to go back to the way things were before — a great, big silence?

He didn't do or say any of those things. He just hugged me.

It was exactly the right thing to do.

We stood that way for a long time. Neither of us said anything — we didn't need to talk after all. The hug said it better.

Finally Dad pulled himself away and took my hand. "Come on," he said. "It's late. You need to sleep. Tomorrow's a big day."

I nodded. He was right. Tomorrow would be a very big day. I promised myself I'd try to make it a good one. I was here, after all, so I might as well.

Luckily it was a fancy bathroom with a sofa in it, the kind that's called a powder room, not a bathroom.

I sat on the sofa and started to cry. The reunion hadn't even begun yet and already everything was going wrong. I wished I hadn't come. I wished I could talk to Carly or Nadia. I wished I had a completely different family, one where there was no divorce.

I stayed there a long time. My eyes were sore from crying and my nose was running. Suddenly I was very tired. All I wanted to do was go to sleep and wake up in my familiar bed in my room at home. Instead I was stuck in a restaurant bathroom in Dallas. What was I going to do?

Someone knocked at the door. I heard Dad's voice. "Amelia, come out. We need to talk."

I didn't want to spend the rest of my life on that sofa, so I got up and opened the door. My knees were stiff and creaky, my cheeks tight with dried tears.

I couldn't look up at Dad or I would start crying again, so I just stood there, staring at his shoes. Now what would happen, I wondered. Would he be mad at me?

But Cleo acted like they were soul sisters. I wanted to gag!

You're so right, Clara. Thanks for understanding!

At least I've already met Justin and his family, so they won't all be new faces.

Poor Amelia won't know anyone.

That was it! I snapped!

"Poor Amelia" is just fine! I don't need to know anyone! I don't want to know anyone! I don't know why I bothered to come!

Clara gave me one of her phony, sugary, oh-I'm-so-concerned-about-you smiles. "What can we do to make this easier for you, Amelia? I understand how hard it must be."

"You don't understand anything!" "None of you do! Just leave me alone!" I threw down my napkin and ran to the bathroom.

Dad avoided the questions about Mom, but he answered most of the other ones. I wonder what he thinks about Mom. (I sure know __her__ opinion of __him__!) He never says anything bad about her, but that doesn't mean he doesn't __think__ those kinds of things.

This is a wonderful opportunity for you girls to get to know your family.

I know it's been far too long without them seeing you — now's our chance to catch up. It'll be fun!

Dad likes to focus on the positive.

Clara nodded and chimed in, "It's a lot of people to meet at once. That may make you nervous, but everyone is very nice. I know exactly how you feel because that's what happened to me, too — I met practically the whole family at the same time!"

I glared at her. She had NO idea how I felt — NONE. The last time I visited she invaded my privacy and READ MY NOTEBOOK!! That's a capital offense as far as I'm concerned and proves my point — if she had __any__ sensitivity at all, she would know better. But she didn't. She doesn't. She's absolutely, totally clueless about my feelings.

Unfortunately that happy mood didn't last long. It would have been nice to just eat dinner and _not_ talk, but Cleo insisted on asking a zillion questions.

I noticed that her table manners hadn't improved, even if the rest of her behavior was fake nicey-nice. I guess it's too hard for her to fake good eating habits.

I have to admit some of her questions were good ones, things I wanted to know too. But mostly I didn't want to think about all the strangers who I was going to meet tomorrow. I didn't want to know whether they liked me or Mom. I could guess the answer about Mom's opinions. I'm pretty sure she hates Dad and everyone he's related to — including Clara and George.

Cleo didn't settle for just the hat
and a kerchief. She went whole hog,
making Dad buy her a plaid shirt,
suede vest, and bright red boots that
clashed with her pink hat. I thought
she looked ridiculous, but Clara said
she was gorgeous, a real Annie Oakley
(whoever that is).

I almost felt sorry for Dad, having
to spend so much money, but he could
have said no. I think he feels guilty
he went so many years without giving us
even a birthday present, so now he's
trying to make up for it. That's fine
with me. I figure I'll wait until I'm 16
and ask for a car. That's way better than
a bunch of goofy cowboy gear.

↑
Cleo the cowgirl—
or is it just Cleo
the cow?

They even had a hat and boots
small enough for George. He
looked SO CUTE! →

George is another reason it's
hard to stay in a bad mood.
when he smiles at you, it's →
impossible not to smile back.

Lassos, chaps, spurs, kerchiefs, boots, saddles, belts, bolo ties, hats, suede jackets and vests with fringe at the bottom — you name it, Roy's had it. They even had chewing tobacco and cowboy gum. With all that, I thought I might see a real cowboy in the store shopping for that special something he just had to own. But all I saw were regular people like us who wanted to pretend to be cowboys for a while.

I never knew there were so many kinds of cowboy hats.

↑
brown ones
with leather
strings

↑
black ones
with silver on
the band

↑
white ones
for the good
guys

↑
pink ones
with bows

I picked a
black one
and a blue
kerchief. →

I thought I
looked good. The
funny thing is,
it's hard to feel
bad with a cowboy
hat on. For some
reason just wearing
it made me feel
better.

I looked like I was ready for an adventure —
a cattle stampede, a thievin' coyote, or a family reunion!
↑

I would rate Dad's mood a white, George's a purple, Clara's a pink, and Cleo's a yellow. And I'm a definite deep, deep black—all before we've been here 24 hours. That's got to be a record for mood busting.

We drove into an enormous parking lot dominated by a huge neon cowboy hat. On the roof of the building next to it was a life-size plastic cow.

Normally this kind of place would put me in a great mood because it seems like an enormous joke. I mean, a real cowboy store? What would they sell besides hats and boots? Lassos? Chaps and spurs? Saddles? Are there real cowboys anymore? Who buys this stuff — tourists like us, or do people here take cowboys more seriously? I mean, you have to wonder.

MOOD MEASURE

On top of the world! Everything's perfect and you're super happy, like you just won the lottery.

You're feeling really good, like nothing can go wrong and the future is one long summer vacation.

You're happy, like you just finished a great book (or, better yet, <u>started</u> one) or ate an ice cream cone.

You haven't had dessert yet but you know it's coming.

You just woke up and the day could go either way. Right now it's not good, but it's not bad, either.

You're a little annoyed, like you stubbed your toe. It's not a big deal — yet!

You're mad enough to yell and snap but not so mad as to throw things.

You're furious, out-of-control angry — steam is coming out of your ears.

You're sad and feel all wilty, like old, limp lettuce.

You're frustrated, like when no matter how many times you explain something, your mom just doesn't get it.

You're sad and mad and frustrated all together. You feel like no one loves you and no one ever will. It's the worst feeling EVER!

When I was little, I had a mood ring that changed colors according to what I was feeling. At least that's what it was supposed to do. Usually it was dark gray or black, even when I was happy. Now I think it was because I have cold hands, but then I thought the colors really meant something. Anyway, moods are much more complicated than the five choices on the mood ring (sad, happy, jealous, angry, in love). If I invented a ring like that, I'd have a way more complicated scale with LOTS more colors.

Basic Moods

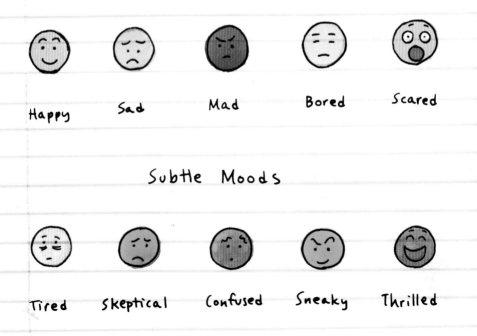

| Happy | Sad | Mad | Bored | Scared |

Subtle Moods

| Tired | Skeptical | Confused | Sneaky | Thrilled |

On the way to the car, Cleo and Clara walked together, whispering back and forth. How did they get to be so buddy-buddy? I suppose I should have been glad because that meant Dad had to walk with me, but I got the feeling he was stuck with me more than wanting to be with me.

It's strange, but with Mom, in the Mom-Amelia-Cleo family, I'm the good daughter, the easier one, and Cleo's the one who exasperates Mom and gets on her nerves. In this family, the Dad-Clara-George-Cleo-Amelia one, I'm the problem child. How did that happen?

↓

I didn't even try to talk to Dad. My mood was going from bad to worse, from black to blacker.

Dad didn't talk to me either. He just talked to George, another "good" child.

But I couldn't say all that without sounding like a brat.
Meanwhile Cleo wore her most angelic face.

It's fine with me to share a bed with Amelia.

I don't mind at all. She can even choose which side she wants.

As if she's the reasonable, nice daughter and I'm NOT!

If I'd known that I'd have to share a bed with Cleo, I DEFINITELY would NOT have come, even if that meant she got to be Dad's favorite. Some things are just not worth it.

But I was already here, so I gritted my teeth and rolled up an extra blanket to go down the center of the fold-out sofa bed. It wasn't the brick wall I wanted, but it was better than nothing.

"Good!" Dad clapped his hands. "I'm glad that's settled. Now we can get our cowboy duds and have some Tex-Mex food for dinner." He used the fake, too-cheery voice he had when we first met. I guess that meant he wasn't comfortable with what was happening.

Good, I thought, glaring at him. I shouldn't be the only one who's miserable. I hope Cleo's snoring is so loud, it keeps him and Clara up all night. That'll show them!

Usually I love hotels, but by the time we got to our room I was in a really bad mood. And it just got worse. We weren't staying in a regular room. It was a suite, so Dad and Clara had the bedroom with a crib put in there for George, and Cleo and I were supposed to sleep in the other room on the sofa bed.

IN THE SAME BED!!!!

There aren't enough exclamation marks in the world to convey how awful that thought was.

I said I could sleep on the floor. I said I could sleep in the bathtub. I said I could even sleep in the lobby — ANYWHERE, so long as I didn't have to share a bed with Cleo.

Clara glared at me. "You're both girls. What's the big deal here? I often shared a bed with my sister when we traveled."

That's you, I thought, not _me_. And that's your sister, NOT Cleo. Here's the problem:

HAZARDS OF CLEO

BRRRR

unpleasant odors from under-the-blanket farts

OW!

cover hogging

scratches from sharp toenails

Cleo, of course, was beaming.

Dad! Clara! Georgie!

She was supernice and polite, like a totally different person. Now I get it — they think they know and like Cleo, but that's not the real Cleo. It's a pod person, a fake.

The whole way to the hotel, Cleo chattered on and on. I just talked to George. No one talked to me.

Until Dad asked me how I liked Dallas. I said I didn't know yet, all I'd seen was highways and billboards (and the cowboy hats and boots in the airport).

"Well, tomorrow we'll see a real slice of Texas. The family reunion is at an old ranch just outside of town. There'll be hay rides and square dancing and, of course, all the barbeque you can eat."

Yeehaw, I thought. But I didn't say it. If Cleo could be polite, so could I.

"Cool!" Cleo said. "Can I get cowboy boots and a cowboy hat? I want to look like a real Texan!"

I snorted. The only thing she would look like was a real jerk.

But Clara thought it was a great idea. "We should all do that," she said. "Don't you agree, Quentin?"

Dad nodded. "That's the spirit. This is going to be the biggest, best family reunion ever — because you girls are here!"

Cleo smiled. I meant to smile. I tried to smile, but it came out all lopsided. Some things you just can't fake.

I'm still not completely comfortable with Dad, but it's a lot easier to be with him now. We're getting used to each other. And now I know that with me first times are usually awkward and tense, not fun and exciting. I just have to remind myself that there's only <u>one</u> first time at a particular thing — after that I've done it before. So no matter how icky this reunion thing is, I might as well get it over with — and the <u>next</u> time I see these people, it'll be <u>much</u> better.

The flight was pretty short and I didn't have to listen to Cleo guffawing for too long when the plane started to land. As soon as we got off the plane, we saw people with cowboy boots and hats. I guess that's how you know you're in Dallas.

Dad was waiting for us, along with Clara and George. At least this time there was no teddy bear.

Cleo!

Amelia!

CLEO! You're so beautiful and grown up now! Amelia, nice to see you.

EE-O! MIA!

Dad had a big smile on his face — he sure wasn't nervous <u>this</u> time. First he hugged Cleo. Then he hugged me. Do I always have to come second in EVERYTHING? At least he was happy to see me — that part was good.

Clara was gushing all over Cleo — it was enough to make me queasy. How come she says Cleo's beautiful and not me?

← Even George was happy to see Cleo. I bet if I'd stayed home, no one would have missed me.

I couldn't help remembering the first time I saw Dad.
There was a strange man waiting for me at the airport in
Chicago and I knew from his jelly-roll nose that he had to
be my dad. I had tried to imagine his face and voice so
many times and there he was, right in front of me. He
wasn't ANYTHING like I'd imagined. I wanted to run
back onto the plane and go home. I wanted to walk
right past him and pick out some other, better guy to be
my dad. But I didn't. I just stood there until he came over
and said, "Hi, you   must be Amelia."

It was SO awkward.

when I →
first saw
him, neither
of us knew
what to say,
we were both
so nervous.

He didn't feel
like a dad to
me, mostly
because I had
no idea how
that would feel.

→

I couldn't
help noticing
how hairy his
hands were,
but I was polite
and shook his
hand anyway.

And he had that
STUPID teddy
bear, like he
was expecting
someone else,
not ME.

That's too bad. He's such a great guy. He's in the 8th grade too so we have a lot in common. Plus he's super cute. You know, I guess it doesn't matter that you two haven't met because you're probably too young to be interesting to him anyway.

Cleo has a knack for the cutting remark - OUCH!

I rolled my eyes. Thanks a LOT, Cleo, I thought. Like you're automatically friends with someone just because they're the same age as you. We all know how true that is! As if the whole 8th-grade class are your friends! And as if I'm automatically boring just because I'm in 6th grade. I'm waaaaay more interesting than Cleo, no matter what! I just have to prove that to Justin — and to everyone else.

Ha! Snort! Guffaw!

I hunkered down in my seat and stared out the window. I tried NOT to pay attention to Cleo's snorts and giggles. No way was I going to ask her what was so funny.

This was going to be the longest weekend ever — and not in a good way. I tried to shut Cleo out. I tried not to think about cousins and uncles and aunts. It was enough worrying about a dad, a stepmom, and a part-time brother.

After all that worrying, it turned out I didn't worry ENOUGH. Mom took us to the airport and we got on the plane and I was just beginning to think that MAYBE this would be a fun trip after all when Cleo took a bunch of papers out of her purse and started reading them. I wouldn't have paid much attention, but she was grinning and laughing — way too happy for ordinary reading. I _had_ to ask her what was so funny.

"Just some e-mails I printed out," she said.

"Why bother to do that? Who are they from?" I asked.

"One of our cousins, Justin. We've been e-mailing and messaging ever since my last visit to see Dad. Didn't you meet him when you went? He's SO sweet!"

My stomach sank. No, I hadn't met him. I had no idea who he was. And now he and Cleo were good buddies and I would be the ONLY person who didn't know anybody. I didn't say anything. I didn't want to admit that Dad had done stuff with Cleo he hadn't done with me (like seeing cousins and aunts and uncles). But I couldn't lie, either, or Cleo would find out.

Hmmm, Justin... that name rings a bell. I think Dad mentioned him, but his family was out of town when I was there so we didn't meet. I think that's what happened.

It may not have been the truth, but it _could_ have been. Why else would Dad not introduce us?

I made up the cousin and aunt stuff because I don't know yet if I have relatives like that. But Carly does, so I know they exist. At least I know George, the cute baby, will be there, so SOMEBODY will be nice to me. And with so many cousins, at least one should be okay.

Finally I added Dad, Clara, Cleo, and me.

I showed Carly my deck of family cards. She laughed but then she said I wasn't being fair — where were all the good types of people? I told her I don't have to worry about __them__. Still, she had a point, so I added a few more cards.

I <u>had</u> to get that image OUT of my head. So I made flash cards of all the possible types of relatives that are NOT Cleo clones. That way I can be on the alert and know who to avoid (and not think of facing a massive crowd of Cleos).

What if Carly's wrong? What if they're not interesting people? What if they're the most BOOOOOORING people on the planet? Or what if they fight and yell a lot? Or are plain annoying like Cleo, talking with their mouths full and singing off-key? What if I'm trapped in a room full of Cleos?! What a nightmare!

Cleos of all ages, boys and girls, in a horrible sing-along

KUMBAYA KUMBAYA!

Grandma Cleos, Grandpa Cleos, baby Cleos, Uncle Cleos, Aunt Cleos, cousin Cleos

HELP!

I'll never survive.

Cleo is totally excited. I'm not so sure. Yeah, I like to see new places and stay in hotels, but not with Cleo. Who can sleep with her snoring? And I'm not crazy about meeting a bunch of strangers. Like I wrote to Nadia, just because they're family doesn't mean I'll like them — or that they'll like me!

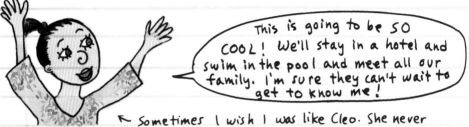

This is going to be SO COOL! We'll stay in a hotel and swim in the pool and meet all our family. I'm sure they can't wait to get to know me!

← Sometimes I wish I was like Cleo. She never worries about anything. And NOTHING embarrasses her.

But I'm not Cleo so I can't help feeling nervous. Carly, my best friend, tried to convince me it would be great. I wish she could come with me — then it __would__ be great. Even if no one else talked to me, I'd have her. Now all I have is Cleo, which is like saying all I have is zero or a negative number.

Amelia, you're going to love it. It's always fun to explore a new city, and you've never been to Dallas. And you'll meet some interesting people, I bet.

Carly thinks my dad is great just because he's a reporter and that's what she wants to be when she grows up. So naturally she thinks the rest of his family is also wonderful. I hope she's right — or at least not __too__ wrong.

So it's all set. Cleo and I will have our first plane trip together with no grown-up around. I hope it's better than sitting next to Cleo on the bus for a field trip — at least then I can open a window to escape her carsick fumes. She'd better **not** get airsick! If she does, I'm spending the whole flight standing in the back of the plane by the toilets (usually not the best-smelling part of an airplane, but compared to puking Cleo, it'll be a breath of fresh air).

I wrote to Nadia about it. She's the one who encouraged me to find my dad in the first place, so in a way she's responsible for all of this happening — meeting Dad, finding a whole new family, the family reunion, all of it.

Dear Nadia,
   Guess what? Cleo and I are going to a big family reunion in Dallas. It's not for Mom's family. It's for Dad's. So I'll meet all these uncles, aunts, and cousins for the first time. And my grandparents! It's strange to think I suddenly have all these people in my life. Except I'm not sure yet if I really do. Just because you're related to someone doesn't mean you have to care about them. So will they care about me? yours till the criss crosses, amelia

Nadia Kurz
61 South St.
Barton, CA
   91010

Naturally Cleo and Clara hit it off. Why didn't I notice it before? Their names are almost the same! I'll just call them the Clones (or the Clowns) from now on.

If Cleo's going, obviously I have to go too - even though having her around will make a bad situation way WORSE. Watching her butter up Clara will give me major indigestion. Still, that's better than watching her butter up Dad. And that's better than staying home and letting her become the favorite daughter while I become the far-away, don't-care-about-her daughter.

Anyway, she can be Clara's favorite. I don't care about that. I want to be George's favorite.

He's such an adorable toddler now. I love the way he walks, like his diaper is weighing him down and making him off-balance. When I kiss him on his belly button, he has the best laugh — it makes me smile deep inside.

He even knows some words. Here's some basic George vocabulary:

↓

Baa - his favorite stuffed lamb

La la - his word for light or lamp

Ni-ni - his word for night-night or go to sleep

Then there's also my grandparents, great-aunts, great-uncles, and cousins once, twice, and thrice removed. It's way too many people to remember. The worst part is they've all known each other their whole lives. Cleo and I don't know ANYBODY! We hardly know our own dad!

I just had a HORRIBLE thought — the only person there I'll feel comfortable with is CLEO!! That can only be an omen of doom!

That's if I go, of course. Mom says we can stay home if we want.

I understand completely if you don't want to go, and I'm sure your father would too.

It's a lot of strange people to have to face all at once. And I do mean strange.

She doesn't sound terribly fond of Dad's family either.

I didn't want to give Mom the satisfaction of convincing me to stay home, but I wasn't sure I wanted to go. Until Cleo gave me no choice.

Of course I'm going! I had a great time last summer when I visited Dad. I can't wait to meet everyone else.

And I really like Clara. She took me to work with her one day and I got to feed some Great Dane puppies. It was so much fun!

③ Something will be broken. Or spilled. Or both.

④ Somebody's feelings will be hurt.

⑤ Something will be forgotten.

It's a different family, but I bet there will still be a bunch of predictable things that happen every time they get together. Without knowing anybody, I can guess what some of those things will be. I'm placing bets with Carly on these. If I'm right, she owes me a banana split.

① Somebody will exclaim how great it is that everyone could come. They will use the word "special" at least five times.

② Some kid will get hurt (not badly) and cry ... and cry.

Okay, it can be painfully boring or embarrassing, but at least I'm used to that kind of family gathering. Now suddenly with my dad I'm part of a HUGE family and in a few weeks I'm going to meet all of them — ALL AT ONCE! They're having an enormous family reunion and, according to Dad, that means Cleo and me now too. What will it be like, facing so many strangers at the same time? It sounds worse than the first day at a new school! I mean, it's one thing to find a place for a dad in my life AND a stepmom AND a half-brother. Now I have to fit in all these other people too? UGH!!

Dad
↓

↑
When I first met him, I thought "Yucch! He looks like Cleo with hairy hands!" But he's like me, too, because we both love to write. He's a reporter for the Chicago Tribune, and when he saw my notebook, he said he'd had one just like it when he was a kid.

George
↓

↑
The first time I saw my baby half-brother, he was about 6 months old. Now he's almost 2 years old and he can walk and talk. He calls me "Mia" because "Amelia" is too hard for him to say, which is better than what he calls Cleo — "Eeoh."

Clara
↓

↑
Dad's second wife (at least I think she's his second one. For all I know he's been married a dozen times). She's a veterinarian, which you would think would make her a super nice person, but you'd be thinking WRONG! She tries way too hard, which just makes her trying.

③ Mom will eat too much dessert and moan about it for the rest of the week.

> I knew I shouldn't have eaten that second piece of pie! See — now my pants don't fit. This whole family is going on a diet starting TODAY!

④ There will be leftovers for at least a week that will reappear at every meal in different disguises.

First, it's string beans almondine. ↓

Then it becomes string bean frittata. ↓

Then it's transformed into mushed bean casserole ↓

Mom thinks that putting lots of cheese on something is enough to make it edible, but some things are too far gone for that.

⑤ Cleo will say SOMETHING that makes me want to sink into the floor. (Actually this happens WAY more often than at family gatherings — it's just more embarrassing then.)

> That reminds me of the time Amelia's bathing suit came off when she tried the high dive. I warned her that bikinis and diving don't mix, but did she listen? Of course not! It was SO FUNNY!!

> Yeah, a real laugh riot.

Looking at that family picture, I can't help noticing that Mom AND both her siblings are single. That can't be a coincidence! One thing's for sure — I'm NOTHING like Mom or Lucy or Frank, so maybe there's hope for me.

The last time we all got together was for Thanksgiving. It was fun to play with Raisa, especially since we hardly ever see her, but mostly it was dull and predictable.

The 5 Things That Happen at Every Family Event

① Uncle Frank will argue with Aunt Lucy about whether fluoride is good for your teeth or a government plot to poison us.

I'm just asking for proof, that's all! Prove to me that fluoride prevents cavities. See, you can't do it! You think it's the fluoride when it's simply the fact that you BRUSH YOUR TEETH! So then why bother with fluoride, eh? Answer me that!

You know, you're a real nut job. Stop drinking tap water if you're so worried about this.

② The main dish — no matter WHAT it is, turkey, meatloaf, brisket, or chicken — will be overcooked and dry.

I don't know what happened this time. I didn't have the oven on too high, I'm sure of that.

Can SOMEONE in this family learn to cook? Every time it's the same thing — a main dish of SAWDUST!

It's a lot to get used to! There's not just Dad, there's his second wife, Clara, not my favorite person in the world, and their baby, George (who, I admit, is one of my favorite people — he's so adorable!). And there's all the family attached to them — aunts, uncles, cousins, grandparents — all of them to consider.

For most of my life, I had a very small family — just me, Cleo, and Mom. When we went to family gatherings, it was still pretty small.

Cleo
↓

↑
She takes up a LOT of space even if she's just one person. She's LOUD and BOSSY and PUSHY.

Mom
↓

↑
She's mostly quiet, not the chattiest person, but once she starts lecturing — WATCH OUT!

Me
↓

↑
I'm the creative spark of the family. Without me, things would be totally out of balance.

↑
Aunt Lucy — she's the opposite of Mom in every way. Mom's super-organized and controlled. Lucy always forgets basic stuff — like packing a toothbrush or leaving the oven on.

↑
Raisa — she's the little girl Aunt Lucy adopted from Russia when she was 3. Now she's 5 and her English is pretty good but she's shy and doesn't say much.

↑
Uncle Frank — like Lucy, he's never been married, and I think I know why. He's one of the most booooring people I've ever met. But he's family, so I have to listen to his dull, dull stories.

Anyway, Carly, my best friend, says no one can understand what goes on in a marriage — the good and the bad — except the people in it. Her parents aren't divorced. They have a really good marriage (at least it looks that way to me, on the outside), but her mom is an expert on broken marriages because that's her job, marriage counseling. (She calls it couples therapy, but it's the same thing.) When I told Ms. Tremain about meeting my dad for the first time (that I can remember), she had some great advice.

Amelia, you need to build your <u>own</u> relationship with your dad based on <u>your</u> experiences with him, not on what your mom says.

Even after all these years, your mom still has a lot of anger and resentment. Without realizing it, she may say things to sabotage your relationship with your dad. That kind of thing can happen.

She also said there was no point in blaming either of them for the past. The question was, what kind of future did I want to have with them? I still can't help being angry about it all, but I'm trying to think about what I want <u>now</u>. That's hard-enough work!

Ever since my visit, my dad's been figuring out how to get me back into his life. I'm figuring out <u>if</u> I want to be there.

Even though he'd remarried and had a baby, my half-brother, George, he didn't know how to be a dad to me. When he picked me up from the airport, he brought me a teddy bear, like I was a baby or something.

NOT what you give an 11-year-old girl. I gave it to George. He liked it. →

He didn't give me what I really wanted — a hug. But we're both better at that stuff now. He tells me he loves me and hugs me. He's better at teasing me and getting my sense of humor. He still has awful taste in clothes when he buys me stuff, but he's learning. And he's told me more about why he left and why he didn't try to see us. Part of it was for our sake, part of it was because Mom was really mad at him.

Mom's version
↓

It was a BIG mistake right from the beginning, but I kept on trying, I really did.

We were seeing a counselor, trying to work things out when you were born. But it all got worse, not better. Quentin wanted out and out he went. I was so ANGRY, I couldn't stand the sound of his voice. I wanted no contact — NONE!

When Mom first told me this, it made me feel terrible, like it was my fault they got divorced. Maybe they could have stayed together if they'd only had one kid to handle. Then I got mad at Mom. Maybe Dad would have helped if she'd let him. I mean, was that fair to Cleo and me?

When I see my dad with George, I think he's a great father. But it makes me sad, too, because he wasn't that kind of father for me. On the plus side, Clara's not that kind of mother for me either. She's just a stepmother (which really means nothing except that she's married to my dad). Mom has her problems, but compared to Clara, she's Mary Poppins.

There are certain things a step-mother should never do. Here's a quick list.

MOTHER

(Yes, a mother can do these things even if you hate it. Come on, she's your mother.)

roll-your-eyes face reserved for moms only

1. Nag you to clean up your room — you don't have to listen, but she has the right to bug you about it.

2. Make embarrassing suggestions about how to clear up your acne, improve your posture, or select a deodorant.

3. Hug and kiss you in public. I know — it's gross. Just remember, other kids' mothers do it to them!

STEPMOTHER

(No, a stepmother can NEVER do this unless you say it's okay. It's YOUR choice, not hers.)

1. Nag you about your grades, studying, tests, homework, ANYTHING to do with school.

2. Tell you about the facts of life — PLEASE! That's what sex ed. in school is for. It's bad enough coming from a parent, but a stepparent — NEVER!

3. Criticize your hair, clothes, taste in music, anything personal that's none of her business.

So I wrote him a letter — actually, a comic strip - telling him I was wondering who he was and why he went away. That was hard, but even harder was waiting for him to answer. Part of me was afraid he wouldn't, part of me was afraid he'd tell me to leave him alone, and a teeny, tiny part of me was hoping he'd tell me how much he loved and missed me.

He didn't do any of those things. When I finally got a letter back, he said he was sorry and wanted to be in my life and he invited me to visit him in Chicago, where he lives. But he didn't say he loved me. He just signed the letter "Dad."

What could I do? I went to Chicago. That was last year. I've seen him a couple of times since then and we e-mail and talk on the phone. I know he's trying to be a good dad, and I'm not mad at him anymore, but I still think he should have been there when I was little. He could have tried. So could have Mom. They both say they have their reasons, but I think they're lame excuses.

Dad's version

↖

Amelia, I'll be honest with you — it was a painful divorce. I needed to travel for my work as a reporter and I couldn't be with your mother as much as she needed. We fought about it for years, long before you were born. We kept hoping things would get better, but they didn't. Once we finally decided to separate, neither of us wanted to see the other one. It was pretty ugly. You and Cleo were both so young, I thought it would be easier if you never knew me.

When we first met in Chicago, he was really nervous. So was I. I didn't know what to expect, what kind of dad he would be, and what it would feel like to call someone "Dad."

↖ Easier on who, I wondered — him or us?

That's what my dad was for most of my life — a big fat question mark. All I knew about him was that he left when Cleo, my sister, was two and I was just a baby. Mom must have been really mad at him because she never told us ANYTHING about him. It was like he didn't even exist. Or maybe _we_ didn't exist for him. I mean, if he wanted to find us, he could have figured out a way. But he didn't.

_I_ was the one who finally found _him_. I nagged and super-nagged Mom until she gave me his name and address.

I was excited to see he actually lived somewhere besides my imagination, but I was also FURIOUS at Mom. She knew where he was ALL ALONG — she just wouldn't tell me or Cleo.

Mom ↘

I don't know why you want to write to him. He's never written to you.

↑ Maybe he DID write to me, but Mom never gave me his letters. How would I know?

All you've ever gotten from him was your name. He picked out Amelia for Amelia Earhart. Don't expect anything or you'll be disappointed.

I'm just saying...

↑ Just because she hates my dad doesn't mean I have to.

Amelia's LONGEST, BIGGEST, MOST-FIGHTS-EVER FAMILY REUNION

by Marissa Moss

(and daughter, sister, half-sister, niece, cousin, stepdaughter, granddaughter Amelia!)

Simon & Schuster Books for Young Readers

New York   London   Toronto   Sydney

which they planned to release near Pearl Harbor. These small subs only had two crew members. Carrying two torpedoes, the midget subs had the potential to cause significant damage to American ships.

On December 5 the strike force was 600 miles north of Oahu. The nervous Japanese pilots wrote letters or tossed restlessly in their bunks as they waited to complete their mission.[6]

3

EARLY
WARNINGS

As the Japanese fleet approached Pearl Harbor, the Americans still had a chance to discover the attack. It would not be easy. There were very few clues, but in the moments before the attack, Americans received early warnings of the Japanese operation. In the waters off of Oahu, American ships discovered Japanese submarines. After the Japanese launched their planes, a radar screen showed the approaching Japanese planes. If the Americans were to discover the Japanese attack, someone would have had to guess what the clues meant.

A Submarine Is Spotted

At about 1 A.M. on December 7, the Japanese submarines neared Pearl Harbor and released the midget subs. Only one of the five made it to Pearl Harbor.

In the early hours of December 7 before the attack, another Japanese midget submarine was involved in an incident. The American destroyer *Ward* and two minesweepers, *Condor* and *Crossbill*, were patrolling the entrance to Pearl Harbor. Suddenly, *Condor*'s officer of the deck, R. C. McCloy, saw what he believed was a submarine periscope. *Condor* sent a report to *Ward*, whose skipper, Lieutenant William W. Outerbridge, was awakened. Outerbridge searched for an hour. He found nothing, and at 4:35 A.M. sent his men back to their bunks. He did not report the incident. Neither did *Condor* or *Crossbill*.

Two hours later Outerbridge was awakened again by a lookout. This time there was no doubt that a small submarine was fifty yards away, and *Ward* attacked it with gunfire and depth charges—explosive devices designed to explode underwater. Depth charges were used throughout the war to destroy submarines.

This time the depth charges worked. The sub, most likely the same one that survived earlier, sank. Outerbridge quickly reported this incident to Pearl Harbor. In his message, at 6:53 A.M., he reported, "We have attacked, fired upon and dropped depth charges upon submarine operating in defensive sea area."[1]

The radio officer on watch at Pearl Harbor was Lieutenant Commander Harold Kaminsky. Kaminsky immediately tried to telephone his superior officers. He had trouble reaching some of them. When he finally reached an officer, the official thought the submarine reports were probably false. Another, the staff duty officer, finally reached Admiral Husband Kimmel at about 7:40 A.M. The admiral decided to wait for verification before doing anything. Despite the attack, Pearl Harbor was not put on alert.

Wreckage of a Japanese midget submarine after the attack on Pearl Harbor.

Radar

Aboard the Japanese carriers, pilots assigned to the first wave of the attack met for a breakfast of rice and red beans. The seas were heavy as big waves rocked the Japanese ships. The air attack commander, Mitsuo Fuchida, would not have allowed his pilots to take off if it had been only an exercise. But 250 miles north of Pearl Harbor, at 6:15 A.M., the 184 planes in the first attack wave took off. One plane crashed into the ocean, but within minutes, the rest were in the air and moving toward Pearl Harbor. The 167 planes in the second wave were then brought on deck, prepared for flight, and about an hour later launched in still rougher seas. A group of fighter planes followed the bombers to provide protection.

In his plane, Fuchida heard a weather report between songs on KGMB and directed his pilots to home-in on the station. The clouds broke at 6:57 A.M., and an almost theatrical red dawn over Oahu filled Fuchida with awe. He knew nothing of the submarine sinking. Nor did he know his planes were on the Americans' radar.

Near the northern tip of Oahu, Private Joseph L. Lockard and Private George E. Elliott operated a mobile radar unit. They were to go off duty at 7:00 A.M., when the unit closed. This Sunday morning, Lockard began to shut down the radar, but Elliott asked him to hold off so he could have some practice using it. Lockard waited, then looked at the screen over Elliott's shoulder. At 7:02 A.M., the two men saw a big blip approaching Oahu from the north. Lockard and Elliott believed the radar blip represented a group of at least fifty planes. Lockard telephoned Lieutenant Kermit Tyler at the Fort Shafter information center to tell him about the blip.

Radar was a new invention in 1941 and still in the experimental stage. The army was still training its operators, and most did not know how to use the equipment. Radar operators could not tell friend from foe and did not even know when Army or Navy flights were coming to Pearl Harbor. No one realized at the time how important radar could be for protecting Pearl Harbor from an air attack.

A Japanese Zero fighter plane is cheered by the Akagi carrier crew as it takes off for Pearl Harbor.

Tyler remembered hearing KGMB's Hawaiian music on his car radio at 3:00 A.M. as he drove to work. A friend had told him the station played music all night long when American B-17 bombers flew in from California. Recalling what his friend had said, Tyler thought the blip represented the bombers coming from California. But the B-17s, then on their way to bolster U.S. forces in the Philippines, were close, but not yet visible on the radar screen. Assuming they were indeed what Lockard and Elliott had picked up on their screen, Tyler simply said to Lockard, "Well, don't worry about it," and did nothing further about the matter.[2]

Lockard argued a little, then gave up and again started to shut down his equipment. Once more Elliott persuaded him to keep it going. The two men watched the blip until they lost it at 7:39 A.M. in echoes from the mountains around them. As the blip finally disappeared, the best chance to warn the Pearl Harbor fleet had been missed.[3]

The morning was unusually beautiful. Far above Opana, Commander Fuchida saw the sun come up and clouds billowing below him. He began to worry whether he and the other pilots would be able to see their target. Then, as he squinted through his binoculars, the clouds parted and he saw the great vessels in Battleship Row and all the other ships glistening in the sun. He thought , "God must be with us!"

At 7:49 A.M., ten minutes after Lockard and Elliott lost their blip, Fuchida signaled the 183 planes in the first wave to attack: *"To, To, To"*—the first syllable of *totsugekiseyo*, the Japanese word for "charge."[4]

4

THE ATTACK

The attack on Pearl Harbor began at 7:56 A.M. on December 7, 1941. As church bells rang and many soldiers and sailors ate their breakfast, Japanese planes descended on Pearl Harbor and the nearby army bases.

Kakeuchi Takahashi, leading the dive bombers, plunged toward the Pearl Harbor Naval Air Station on Ford Island and dropped the first bomb. It hit a seaplane ramp, sending up a shower of water and mud.

Rear Admiral William Furlong saw the bomb falling. He was waiting for breakfast on the quarterdeck of his flagship *Oglala*, an old minelayer. Furlong thought an American pilot had dropped the bomb accidentally. Then Takahashi banked and the admiral saw the rising sun emblems on the plane's wings. "Japanese! Man your stations!" Furlong shouted.[1]

At the same moment, Lieutenant Commander Logan Ramsey, standing at a window of the Ford Island command center, saw the bomb explode and ran to the radio room. He ordered the operators to broadcast on all frequencies in plain English, "Air raid, Pearl Harbor. This is NOT drill!"[2] At 7:58 A.M., this message went to the commander of Pearl Harbor, Admiral Husband

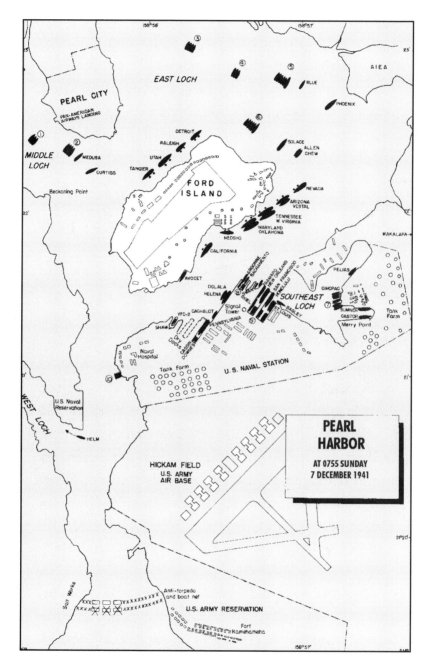

Pearl Harbor the morning of December 7, 1941.

Kimmel, to Washington, and to the headquarters of the United States Asiatic Fleet in the Philippines.

In Washington, where it was 1:30 P.M., the Ford Island message was brought to Secretary of the Navy Frank Knox, who exclaimed, "My God! This can't be true, this must mean the Philippines!" Assured that it was indeed Pearl Harbor, Knox telephoned the White House, where President Roosevelt was with Harry Hopkins, his closest civilian aide. Hopkins, a former secretary of commerce, was also surprised. "Surely Japan would not attack in Honolulu," he said. But Roosevelt said he thought "it was just the kind of unexpected thing the Japanese would do."[3]

Battleship Row

The main targets for the Japanese attack were the eight battleships. *Nevada, Arizona, West Virginia, Tennessee, Oklahoma, California,* and *Maryland* were moored in "Battleship Row," and *Pennsylvania* was in dry dock across the channel. The Japanese had hoped to destroy the three American aircraft carriers, but none was in Pearl Harbor that day. By good fortune one aircraft carrier, *Enterprise,* and several other ships were delayed returning to Pearl Harbor by rough weather and narrowly missed the attack.

The first wave of Japanese planes wasted little time and took advantage of the surprise. Some planes, equipped with torpedoes that could go through the water and explode when they hit a ship, approached their targets just fifty feet in the air. The planes launched the torpedoes and quickly flew away to prepare for a second run. All the battleships on Battleship Row were hit by torpedoes.

Another group of dive bombers and horizontal bombers attacked in many waves. Horizontal bombers dropped their bombs from high in the air, away from American anti-aircraft fire. Dive bombers flew high, but dove toward their target, dropped their bombs, and then flew away. Bombs from both kinds of planes hit battleships as well as other ships and army bases around Pearl Harbor.

Arizona

In the seconds before the Japanese attacked, Marine Major Alan Shapley enjoyed a big breakfast on the battleship *Arizona*. As coach and first baseman of the ship's baseball team, he was looking forward to the fleet championship game that afternoon. Shapley had not finished his pancakes when he heard a loud bang and ran out on deck. Some sailors at *Arizona*'s rail were watching planes race across the harbor, circling in figure 8's and dropping bombs. One of the sailors said admiringly: "This is the best . . . drill the Army Air Force has ever put on!"[4]

Fifteen-year-old Seaman Martin Mathews, who had lied about his age when he enlisted, was visiting with a friend on *Arizona* when they heard the first bomb explosions. The General Quarters alarm sounded, telling everybody to go to the battle stations, but Mathews did not know what to do. He normally worked at the Ford Island Naval Air Station. "I had no place to go," he remembered. "I didn't even know what General Quarters was. So I just stayed in the back part of the ship. Pandemonium broke loose; sailors were running everywhere. It was a state of confusion."[5]

Explosions kept hitting the *Arizona*, rocking the ship, and Mathews suddenly found himself in the water. *Arizona* had been hit by a bomb that landed on one of its guns and blew up the forward magazine where shells and explosives were stored. The explosion killed nearly 1,000 men and sent many more flying into the water. Within minutes, *Arizona* was in flames and sinking. After swimming to a nearby buoy, Mathews recalled seeing "steel fragments in the air, fire, oil—God knows what all—pieces of timber, pieces of boat deck, canvas, and even pieces of bodies. . . . It's far too much for a boy of fifteen years old to have seen."[6]

When general quarters was sounded on *Arizona*, Shapley went up the ladder to his post, a fire control station on the mainmast, but the ship was already on fire. Shapley ordered his men to go back down and save themselves. When the bomb hit the forward magazine, he was sent hurtling into the water, partly paralyzed by the shock and without his clothes, which were blown off by the explosion.

Earl Nightengale was also in the water. He tried to swim but could not. Following the explosion oil leaked into the harbor and many sailors found it difficult to swim in the oily water. Shapley, who had begun to recover from the shock and was able to swim, seized Nightengale by the shirt and told him to hang onto his shoulders. The exhausted Shapley soon had to pause. Nightengale let go and told the major to go on alone but Shapley refused. Somehow finding the strength, he pulled Nightengale to safety.

When they finally made it ashore on Ford Island, some of their badly burned shipmates were already there, "moaning and walking around in a daze" from the shock, Shapley recalled. He wandered around himself,

The Arizona *is seen sinking following the explosion of the forward magazine.*

still naked, until someone gave him some clothing and a glass of whiskey.[7]

Arizona's senior surviving officer, Samuel Fuqua, helped the few others who survived to leave the ship. Earl Pecotte, ordered by Fuqua to jump off, asked Fuqua if he himself was going to swim ashore. "Not until the Japs leave," was the reply. He won the Medal of Honor.[8]

On shore, Admiral Kimmel was on the telephone when a sailor rushed in to tell him: "There's a message from the signal tower saying the Japanese are attacking Pearl Harbor and this is no drill!"[9] Kimmel hung up and hurried outside where he watched in anguish the destruction of *Arizona*. Fewer than 200 of *Arizona*'s 1400-person crew survived the attack.

Nevada

Tied up near *Arizona*, the battleship *Nevada* was threatened by the *Arizona*'s flames. *Nevada* was also under attack from above. *Nevada*'s antiaircraft battery fired back under directions from twenty-one-year-old Ensign Joseph K. Taussig, Jr. Taussig's left leg had been shattered by a missile, but it did not stop him. After he shot down one torpedo plane, another plane successfully hit *Nevada*. The ship began to lean to one side, as water poured into the hole created by the torpedo. Below deck, the ship's crew flooded the other side of the ship and saved the *Nevada* from turning over on its side.

The senior officer on board *Nevada*, Lieutenant Commander Francis Thomas, decided the ship should try to escape despite the flooding. Chief Boatswain Edwin J. Hill directed the casting-off of *Nevada*'s lines from the pier, then jumped in the water and swam back to his ship.[10] The *Nevada* started moving down the channel. A battleship normally needs a couple of hours to light its boilers, but fortunately Taussig had lit the boilers just before the attack. In this case the ship's two boilers enabled it to get steam up and start moving—without tugboats—past burning and sunken ships within forty-five minutes.

Japanese Commander Fuchida was circling above the harbor, taking pictures of the damage, when he saw the *Nevada* steaming out of Pearl Harbor. He quickly realized that if *Nevada* were sunk, the battleship would block the channel. As the second Japanese attack wave arrived, including seventy-eight dive bombers that were ordered to destroy all the ships that had survived the first wave. Many of the bombers swarmed down on the battleship. Thomas moved *Nevada* out of the channel and onto Hospital Point, where he grounded it. As Chief Boatswain Hill went forward to drop anchor, three bombs dropped near the bow and he disappeared, never to be seen again. He was later awarded the Medal of Honor.[11]

West Virginia

While the *Tennessee* escaped with little damage, the nearby *West Virginia* was not so lucky. Captain Mervyn

"above and beyond the call of duty"

DORIE MILLER
Received the Navy Cross
at Pearl Harbor, May 27, 1942

A Navy recruitment poster celebrating the heroism of Doris (Dorie) Miller.

Bennion was on the signal bridge when he was hit by a piece of flying metal from a bomb explosion. Mess Attendant Doris Miller, an African American man who worked in the kitchen, was summoned to carry the captain to safety below, but flames blocked the way. Miller finally helped to carry him to a sheltered spot on the navigation bridge. Bennion did not want to leave the bridge. Still conscious, though near death, the captain insisted that his crew leave him and save themselves.

After putting the captain down, Doris Miller picked up a machine gun and began firing. He later helped Lieutenant (jg) Frederick White haul wounded men through oil and seawater, "unquestionably saving the lives of a number of people who might otherwise have been lost."[12] In 1941 the United States Navy did not allow African Americans to serve except as kitchen attendants. Miller was the first African American to win the Navy Cross and his heroic story helped end segregation in the Navy.

Oklahoma

When five torpedoes hit the battleship *Oklahoma*, there was no time to try to save the ship. Because the lower compartments had been left open for an expected inspection on Monday, the ship rapidly flooded. As men rushed to their battle stations in the darkness, *Oklahoma* capsized. Many of the crew members were trapped inside, but others escaped by climbing over the upturned hull.

As the ship turned over and the water in the compartments rose, many crewmen drowned. Lieutenant (jg) Aloysius Schmitt, a Catholic chaplain, started out a washroom porthole but a prayer book in his pocket caught in the frame. He backed off, then others started through. Schmitt pushed four of them through the opening and was still in the compartment when water filled it completely. Schmitt was not the only one to sacrifice his own life to help others escape. Seaman James Ward and Ensign Francis Flaherty stayed inside a darkened gun turret as the vessel capsized and held flashlights so their shipmates could save themselves.

Many people tried to save the *Oklahoma* crew. Holes were cut in the sides of *Oklahoma* to rescue the trapped men. As the water rose, others tapped on the steel bulkhead with wrenches to draw attention. They hoped that by making noise, rescue workers would know where to cut the holes. The haunting tapping lasted for hours after the attack. Some people were rescued, but many others died in the ship.[13]

One survivor of the *Oklahoma*, Seaman Stephen B. Young, was certain that he would die. Young remembered the anger he felt: "Why couldn't we have died in the sun where we could have met death head on? That was the way to die, on your feet, like a man."[14]

California

Several torpedoes struck *California* at 8 A.M. and ten minutes later the battleship's power went out as water

Sailors search for survivors. The capsized Oklahoma *can be seen in the background.*

poured through the holes into the fuel tanks. In one flooded compartment Robert Scott was at his battle station at a compressor feeding air to *California*'s antiaircraft gun crew. Scott was ordered to leave but refused. "As long as I can give these people air, I'm sticking," he said. He did and it cost him his life.[15]

Herbert Jones set up a group to supply ammunition to *California*'s antiaircraft battery. Mortally wounded, he refused to be removed. Thomas Reeves also passed ammunition to the battery until he was killed. Jackson Pharris moved ammunition and pulled men to safety from the battery's flooded compartment. Badly injured and twice overcome by oil and fumes, he somehow survived—the only one of the four to do so. Scott, Jones, Reeves and Pharris all won the Medal of Honor for their heroism that day.

The Airfields

The battleships were not the only targets for the Japanese attack. Japanese bombers attacked the nearby Kaneohe Naval Air Station, Hickam Field, Wheeler Field, Ewa Field, and Bellows Field. Bombers and fighter planes attacked these bases to stop Americans from launching a counter-attack. As on the battleships, most people at these bases were completely surprised by the attack. At the Naval Air Station on Ford Island damage and casualties were relatively light because the combat planes were with their carriers at sea, but the other air fields were not so lucky.

Hickam Air Depot

Sixty-five bombers were based at Hickam Field. The bombers had been parked close together, neatly lined up so they could be more closely guarded against sabotage but helpless against an air attack. "There was confusion," a survivor recalled, "plus when the attack came men were completely petrified and frightened stiff."[16] Most of the bombers were destroyed. Hangars and barracks were attacked with gunfire from low-flying planes as well.

At Hickam, Robert Crouse and others awaited the arrival of the B-17s from California. At first Crouse thought the smoke above the harbor came from a navy drill. But the planes came closer, and machine guns began firing. Bombs dropped. Some men with pistols shot vainly at the planes, others took cover. Crouse was wounded in the ankle and crawled into a hangar. It did not seem safe there so he got under a tractor until the first attack wave had gone. Then, bleeding badly, he dragged himself out and was picked up by a soldier using his car as an ambulance for four or five wounded men. A lieutenant aboard, Crouse recalled, "kept us amused by 'cussing' every bump and the driver

Extensively damaged fighter planes following the bombing of Wheeler Field.

alternately." Crouse met him again on a ship going back to the mainland and learned that the lieutenant who had sustained their spirits had lost both legs.[17]

A doctor at Hickam noticed that the clothing of Carmen Calderon, who helped carry the wounded, was soaked in blood. The doctor insisted that Calderon undress for an examination. He found Calderon had been carrying the men with a broken arm. Hickam's casualties were the largest of any army post on that day: 158 dead or missing, 336 wounded.[18]

Wheeler

A United States fighter force of 140 planes was based at Wheeler Field in central Oahu. Just as at Hickam, all were parked close together so guards could protect them from possible sabotage. And just as at Hickam, they made an excellent target for the Japanese. At two minutes past 8 A.M., twenty-five dive bombers destroyed most of them. The bombers also attacked Schofield Barracks, the infantry post next to Wheeler, as well as tents where crewmen slept.

Kaneohe Naval Air Station

Kaneohe Naval Air Station endured three attacks. The first came at 7:45 A.M. as the marine guard was assembled for the morning flag-raising ceremony. Patrol planes, fueled, fully armed, and parked together, were set on fire. Eighteen more Japanese planes, most of them dive bombers, joined in the second attack. In the third attack, a bomb exploded in a hangar, killing

Kaneohe Naval Air Station sailors attempt to save a burning plane.

several men trying to get ammunition stored there. As a result of all three attacks, every plane on the base was destroyed or badly damaged.

During the attack, John Finn, picked up a machine gun from one of the parked planes and began blazing away. Wounded in his stomach, chest, arms and foot, he kept on firing until he was ordered to cease. "It was not my day to die," he said years later. "I was so hopping mad, I wanted to shoot every . . . plane out of the sky."[19] He, too, was rewarded the Medal of Honor.

Ewa Field

Ewa Field was attacked by twenty Japanese fighters. After demolishing the aircraft on the field, they shot at personnel. Among the wounded was the base commander, Claude Larkin. Even after getting wounded, Larkin organized the Ewa defenses, which consisted mostly of rifles and .30-caliber machine guns from damaged planes. A second attack at Ewa came at 8:35 A.M. and a third between 9 and 9:30 A.M. By the end, none of the forty-seven planes on the base could fly.

Bellows Field

Bellows Field, a small base a few miles southeast of Kaneohe, had received phone calls from Hickam Field and from Kaneohe with reports of the attacks. In fact, Hickam had asked for and received fire fighting equipment from Bellows. So it is puzzling that when Bellows itself was attacked just before 8:30 A.M., no one was prepared. Private Raymond McBriarty saw a lone Japanese plane buzzing the field and continued on his way to chapel services. One of the B-17s from California, on its way to the Philippines, made a forced landing near the chapel, and at 9 A.M. about nine low-flying Japanese planes made a serious attack. The air raid signal finally sounded, and the chapel emptied as men rushed to their stations.

McBriarty picked up a gun, mounted it in a parked plane, and fired at the Japanese planes. When they left, he took off after them in the plane, but engine trouble forced him to abandon the chase.

A Japanese bomber flying over Pearl Harbor.

One Bellows officer, Phillip Willis, slept through the first attack, having returned just before dawn from an off-base party. The second attack woke him up. Still in his tuxedo trousers and shirt, he put on his helmet, flight jacket, and a pair of cowboy boots, and ran to the runway. When he got there, he saw a fighter pilot hampered by his parachute pack as he tried to climb into his cockpit. Willis ran to the plane to help the pilot. While there, Japanese machine-gun fire hit the plane and killed the pilot. Willis was saved by the parachute, which stopped the bullets from hitting him.[20]

Solace

To care for the many wounded, there were two hospitals ashore and a hospital ship in the harbor, *Solace*, which rapidly became an emergency ward. Nurses bathed and bandaged the wounded and helped the dying. They did not even look up when loudspeakers warned of enemy planes zooming above. The hospital ship was repeatedly rocked by bombs and nurses soon became covered with blood as they cared for the wounded amid the rat-a-tat-tat of machine guns and other weapons. It seemed that the Japanese were flying close to the hospital ship to protect themselves from the American antiaircraft fire.[21]

The nurses on *Solace* worked under Chief Nurse Grace Lally. Lally had been in the navy twenty years. In 1938 she had helped evacuate American women and children from China following the Japanese invasion. Seeing the courage of the wounded at Pearl Harbor, she was determined that people on *Solace* would have a Christmas, with presents (from the Red Cross) and a decorated tree atop the mast. They did. In the first twenty months of the war in the Pacific, 7,500 casualties were treated aboard *Solace*. Only sixteen men died.[22]

Confused Friendly Fire

A little after 6 A.M. the aircraft carrier *Enterprise* sent eighteen American dive bombers to scout the area between his task force and Pearl Harbor. Later he was informed of the message from Ford Island about the raid.

"My God!" Admiral William Halsey said. "They're

shooting at my own boys—tell [Admiral Husband] Kimmel!"[23]

Halsey's "boys" were indeed being shot at—by Japanese pilots as well as by confused Americans on the ground. One *Enterprise* pilot, Manuel Gonzales, shouted over the radio: "Don't shoot—I'm a friendly plane!" Gonzales and his plane were never seen again. Six *Enterprise* planes were shot down, at least one by American gunfire. Six others landed at Ewa Field, the Marine air base west of Pearl Harbor.[24]

The dozen B-17s on their way from California had been sent to help American forces in the Philippines, under the command of General Douglas MacArthur. The planes were unarmed so they could carry more fuel for the long fourteen-hour flight. The Hickam Field base commander had been waiting for them since 6 A.M. but they had been delayed by a navigation error. They approached Oahu shortly after 8 A.M., completely unaware of the attack on Pearl Harbor.

As they did, Major Truman Landon, in command of the American planes, saw other planes flying toward him and assumed they were friendly. When he saw the rising sun on the wings he immediately knew something was wrong. "Those are Japs!" he shouted over his intercom.[25]

Many Americans on the ground, thinking the American planes were part of the Japanese attack, fired at them. But somehow all the American bombers managed to land, although several were in bad shape and one was destroyed.

5

A DEVASTATING LOSS

One of the duties of the Japanese flight leader was to assess the damage at Pearl Harbor for a report to Admiral Chuichi Nagumo, who headed the strike force. Commander Fuchida rejoiced at the task. Through the heavy smoke he had counted seven battleships sunk or badly damaged, a cruiser crippled, all the Hawaiian airfields in flames, and almost no American aircraft in the skies.

The toll was more devastating than Fuchida realized. Five battleships were sunk and three others heavily damaged. Three cruisers and six auxiliary vessels were damaged, and four destroyers put out of action. A total of twenty-one vessels were sunk or damaged. Only the navy's submarines survived the attack undamaged.

The ships at Pearl Harbor, at least, fought back. Most of the planes did not: they were parked on the ground, wingtip to wingtip. Admiral Kimmel and General Short believed that was the best way to guard against sabotage. As a result, the airplanes were easy targets for the Japanese attack. According to some estimates the Navy lost 80 planes—more than half its total in Hawaii. Of 234 Army aircraft, 97 were written off as lost.

The toll in American lives was also high, although no one is sure exactly how many died. The Navy and Marine Corps apparently had 3,077 killed, 960 missing, and 876 wounded. The Army casualties were 226 killed and 396 wounded. Most of the Navy and Marine dead were on *Arizona*, as were most of the missing. The Navy lost three times as many men as it had lost from enemy action in two previous wars—the Spanish-American War and World War I.[1]

There were many wounded. The staff at Pearl Harbor Naval Hospital treated 545 battle casualties, 350 of them with extensive body burns. At the Army's Tripler General Hospital at Fort Shafter, the wives and daughters of servicemen helped treat the patients as did civilian employees and civilian doctors and nurses.

Civilians, in fact, were quite well prepared for disaster: Honolulu officials had established the Major Disaster Council in June 1941 to handle crises. The council had set up a system using private trucks as emergency ambulances.

Japanese losses were relatively minor. One dive bomber, five torpedo planes, and three fighters were lost in the first wave. Six fighters and fourteen dive bombers were shot down from the second wave, when the defenders were somewhat better prepared. Only fifty-five Japanese airmen were lost in action.

Fuchida was eager to attack again. He wanted another crack at the airfields and a chance to sink more ships. He appealed to Nagumo to allow him to lead a third air strike. Nagumo, however, worried about the American's ability to counter-attack. Where were the absent aircraft carriers? Both Fuchida and Nagumo realized these ships could be pursuing the Japanese strike force. In fact, the American aircraft carrier, *Enterprise*, was searching for the Japanese fleet. Nagumo believed his mission had been accomplished. Why risk bigger losses? When Fuchida realized there would be no third raid, he saluted the admiral without speaking and walked off angrily.[2]

The decision not to attack again spared the Navy's ship repair shops and oil tanks, which Fuchida had noticed but had not bombed. Destruction of those two targets would have made the American defeat far greater. The oil tanks held 4.5 million gallons. After the war Admiral Kimmel testified that if they had been destroyed, "It would have forced the withdrawal of the fleet to the coast."[3] The tanks' loss, according to Commander Edwin T. Layton, Kimmel's intelligence officer, would have kept the American carrier forces from operating in the western Pacific for more than six months.

The intact repair shops enabled the Navy to do an outstanding job of restoring most of the damaged ships under conditions that were incredibly difficult and dangerous. A combination of fuel oil and seawater flooded most of the sunken battleships, making it necessary for repair workers to spend 20,000 hours underwater.[4]

Because it would be months before ships then under construction in California and elsewhere could be completed, speed in repairs was essential. One remarkable example was *Nevada*. Lieutenant Commander Francis Thomas had intentionally grounded that battleship when it was under attack. His action kept the harbor channel open, allowing the Navy to continue using Pearl Harbor. The ship was almost entirely flooded and hydrogen sulfide, a deadly gas, had accumulated in the steering engine room, killing two men and overcoming six others.

Nevada was refloated on February 12 and before the end of 1942 was back in service. Of the other battleships, *California* was restored to duty in 1943, and *West Virginia* joined the war effort in 1944. Much time and money were spent on *Oklahoma* before it was decided it could not be rehabilitated. *Oklahoma* was finally sold as scrap metal in 1944. While being towed to the mainland it sank at sea in a storm.[5]

Utah and *Arizona* still rest at the bottom of Pearl Harbor. A memorial spanning *Arizona*'s hull was built in 1962. Those who have visited the memorial have found it a moving experience.

Luck, both good and bad, played a part in the Pearl Harbor disaster. Because some B-17s were flying toward Oahu at the same time as the Japanese planes, the radar blip betraying the attackers was disregarded. And a last-minute alert sent by The Chief of Staff,

The sunken destroyer Downes *after the attack.*

General George Marshall to both Short and Kimmel before the attack did not arrive until long after it had begun, for a variety of mischances.

Destiny — or luck — may have played a part in still another circumstance: the location of the American battleships. They could all have been at sea, where Kimmel had considered sending them a short time before the attack. Had they been discovered and attacked in deeper waters, their sinking would have been a calamity. "It was God's divine will," Admiral Chester Nimitz, who replaced Kimmel as Pacific Fleet commander, said later.[6]

6

THE AFTERMATH

Immediately after the attack on Oahu, anger and determination were mixed with confusion and fear. Rumors quickly spread that the Japanese would invade Hawaii. The loyalty of the territory's 160,000 Japanese residents came immediately into question.

At the Punahou elementary school, there were American and Japanese students. One American, Martha Branneman, remembered at least one Japanese teacher—Mr. Wattanbe—as "wonderful." The children—Japanese and non-Japanese—continued to play together after the attack, she recalled in an atmosphere of "genuine caring for each other."[1]

General Short, however, warned Hawaii's governor, Joseph B. Poindexter, that uprisings by Japanese residents were likely. The general persuaded Poindexter to proclaim martial law over all Hawaii, putting the army in control of all aspects of civilian life. Schools were closed and the sale of liquor was banned for months.

The day after the attack "Japanese paratroopers" in dungarees were reported to have landed on Oahu. At the Kaneohe Air Station, sailors were ordered to change from dungarees into whites dyed (with coffee) a deep brown. Then came a corrected report: The invaders wore khakis, change to whites. Next came another report: The invaders wore white. A new order followed: All hands, back to dungarees![2]

That evening, John Garcia, a young Hawaiian worker at the Pearl Harbor Navy Yard, drove a truckload of marines a few miles into the valley where the Japanese paratroopers were said to have landed. A total blackout, ordered by authorities, was in effect. Suddenly the lights went on at a house in the valley and the marines started shooting at it. The lights quickly went out. There were no paratroopers.

On the mainland, the feeling in some areas, especially on the West Coast, was not far from panic. Three air-raid alerts were sounded in San Francisco on the night after the attack. Mayor Fiorello LaGuardia of New York warned of the possibility of an attack on the East Coast.

War Declared

On December 8, President Franklin Roosevelt asked Congress for a declaration of war against Japan. His five minute speech was broadcast nationwide on radio. Few of the millions who heard it ever forgot it. Both houses of Congress approved the war declaration with only one vote against war.

Before Pearl Harbor many Americans opposed involvement in a war. The "sneak attack" by Japan changed things. The nation was swept by a wave of patriotism. It would be an exaggeration to say that the isolationist movement died overnight, but it came close to just that. One prominent isolationist, former President Herbert Hoover, said shortly after the attack: "American soil has been treacherously attacked by Japan. Our decision is clear. It is forced upon us. We must fight with everything we have."[3] It was a demonstration of the sudden change in mood caused by the attack. Newspapers across the country expressed anger and determination to fight.[4]

At the time of Pearl Harbor there were a million and a half men in the United States Army, and a million of them were still in training. To thousands of young men hearing about the attack there was no doubt about what to do. They went directly to a service headquarters to enlist. Sometimes they joined a line several blocks long. Many were told they already had a draft notice from the president of the United States informing them they were to be inducted into the army.

One of these men, Elliot Johnson of Portland, Oregon, soon found himself in a new world where discipline was the key word. But he was happy because "we were fighting to save the free world and keep it free."[5]

More than fifteen million men served in the United States armed forces during World War II. More than 300,000 of them were killed, including 36,000 in the

Navy and 19,000 in the Marine Corps. In contrast, 1.2 million Japanese servicemen were killed in battle.

Following the attack on Pearl Harbor everything changed. "There was a complete change in attitude," explained William Pefley who worked at the navy yard in Portsmouth, Virginia. "We weren't just helping England [fight against Germany] anymore; we were helping ourselves. Now it was our war. So everybody decided: 'No matter what the hours may be, let's get the ships out. Whatever we can do to help this war effort, we are going to do.'"[6]

Two days after the attack President Roosevelt delivered a second radio address. Roosevelt warned that America faced a great challenge. To meet that challenge, the president said, the American people would have to live with many shortages. Gasoline, sugar, meat, and other things would have to be rationed. Higher taxes, smaller profits, longer working hours, and dangerous duty in the army and navy lay ahead.[7]

War in Europe

On December 11, Germany declared war on the United States. Winston Churchill, the British Prime Minister, was relieved to know that the United States would now help fight against Germany. England needed more than American supplies, England needed American soldiers. The need for a conference seemed urgent, so Churchill came to Washington on December 22, 1941, and stayed for three weeks. The United States joined England and the other "Allied"

ADDRESS OF THE PRESIDENT
TO THE CONGRESS OF THE UNITED STATES
BROADCAST FROM THE CAPITOL, WASHINGTON, D.C.
December 8, 1941 -- 12.30 P.M., E.S.T.

MR. VICE PRESIDENT, AND MR. SPEAKER, AND MEMBERS OF THE SENATE AND HOUSE

OF REPRESENTATIVES: (TO THE CONGRESS OF THE UNITED STATES:)

Yesterday, December 7, 1941 -- a date which will live in infamy
-- the United States of America was suddenly and deliberately attacked by
naval and air forces of the Empire of Japan.

The United States was at peace with that nation and, at the
solicitation of Japan, was still in conversation with its Government and
its Emperor looking toward the maintenance of peace in the Pacific. Indeed,
one hour after Japanese air squadrons had commenced bombing in the American
Island of Oahu, the Japanese Ambassador to the United States and his col-
league delivered to (the) our Secretary of State a formal reply to a recent
American message. And while this reply stated that it seemed useless to continue the existing diplomatic negotiations, it contained no threat or hint
of war or of armed attack.

It will be recorded that the distance of Hawaii from Japan makes
it obvious that the attack was deliberately planned many days or even weeks
ago. During the intervening time the Japanese Government has deliberately
sought to deceive the United States by false statements and expressions
of hope for continued peace.

The attack yesterday on the Hawaiian Islands has caused severe
damage to American naval and military forces. I regret to tell you that
very many American lives have been lost. In addition American ships have
been reported torpedoed on the high seas between San Francisco and Honolulu.

Yesterday the Japanese Government also launched an attack against

*The first part of President Roosevelt's speech before
Congress declaring war against Japan.*

countries in their fight against Germany, Italy, and now Japan. American defeats continued in the Pacific. The need for more ships, planes, and munitions in the Pacific concerned the president, but he also promised to help the British defeat Germany. President Roosevelt and Churchill had been friends for several years, but were now closer than ever. Churchill telegraphed from the White House: "We live here as a big family in the greatest intimacy and informality, and I have formed the very highest regard and admiration for the president." As a consequence of their friend-ship, the wartime alliance between the two nations became extraordinarily effective.[8]

Boom on the Homefront

After Pearl Harbor the government spent vast sums of money to buy new weapons for the military. The entire automobile business was converted to the production of munitions. This caused 44,000 auto dealers and their 400,000 employees to be laid off. However, plenty of jobs were available and unemployment all but vanished. New defense factories sprang up across the country like mushrooms. Older plants were put to new use. A corset factory began making grenade belts. A factory that made pinball machines produced armor-piercing shells. In aircraft plants farm girls learned how to rivet, and at navy yards they learned how to weld. Five million women joined the civilian work force from 1941 to 1943. The total work force increased by

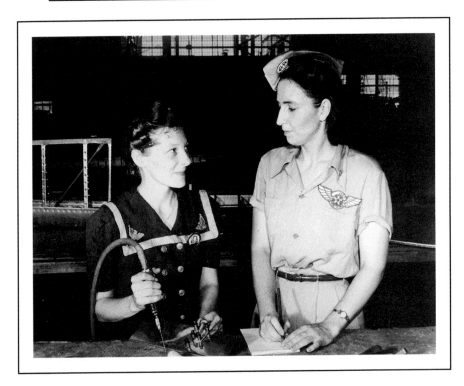

After Pearl Harbor many women worked in war industries.

7 million during the war, to more than 53 million in
1945.

Early in January Roosevelt warned Congress and
the people in his State of the Union message that "the
news is going to get worse and worse before it begins
to get better," and that he would have to ask again for
sacrifices. New production goals had to be set. Those
he listed for 1942 included: 60,000 planes, 45,000
tanks, 20,000 anti-aircraft guns, 6 million tons of mer-
chant shipping. These figures, considered astronomical
at the time, "will give the Japanese and the Nazis a

little idea of just what they accomplished at Pearl Harbor," Roosevelt said as Congress cheered.[9]

New military bases were rapidly built, and millions of families moved to overcrowded production centers. Shantytowns sprang up. There were so few beds in some places that they were rented out in three shifts a day. Eventually, however, defense factory workers got $100 million worth of new housing.

Workers' wages, boosted by overtime, came to far exceed what they had previously been a short time earlier. William Pefley recalled: "Going to work in the navy yard after coming out of the machine shops in

Soon after Pearl Harbor, the United States began to produce new planes, ships, and weapons. The F6F *Hellcat, shown here, was faster, more heavily armed and better protected than its Japanese counterpart, the Zero.*

Pennsylvania, I felt like something had come down from heaven. I went from forty cents an hour to a dollar an hour." Like many, Pefley was driven by more than simply the desire to increase his pay: "[I]t was very important that we got every single ship that came in [for repairs] out quickly so they'd be fighting again. . . . Many a time the men would work eight hours and you needed some of them, the experienced ones, to get the ship out on time. So we'd ask who would care to work straight through. And just about everybody there would volunteer and work until they could almost go to sleep. . . . Your best friend might be out there on one of those ships, maybe getting bombed."[10]

Difficult living conditions, shortages, high taxes all brought grumbles, which were met with the universal rejoinder "Don't you know there's a war on?" The result of all the effort was that America produced more than 300,000 planes, 87,000 warships, 102,000 tanks, and 47 million tons of artillery ammunition.

Suspicion on Both Sides

Following the attack on Pearl Harbor, many Americans worried about the threat of sabotage posed by Japanese Americans. Everyone was caught up in the suspicion. After a trip to Pearl Harbor, Secretary of the Navy Frank Knox said he believed the attack had succeeded largely because of sabotage. No evidence of sabotage was ever found.

Suspicion of Japanese and Japanese Americans was high throughout the war. The *Los Angeles Times* put it this way: "A viper is nonetheless a viper wherever the egg is hatched—so a Japanese-American, born of Japanese parents, grows up to be a Japanese, not an American."[11]

Finally, in 1942, President Roosevelt decided to send 110,000 Japanese-Americans to live in "detention centers." More than 70,000 were American citizens. The homes, jobs, and property of these people were taken away and they were forced to live in ten fenced-in prison camps. The living quarters were in tar-papered wooden barracks containing one-room apartments furnished with cots, blankets, and a light bulb. Meals were unpleasant and there was little medical care. In one case, two thousand Japanese-Americans were kept in a single building in a stockyard in Portland, Oregon, sleeping there on sacks filled with straw.[12]

For the United States and its allies, the first six months of the war in the Pacific were dark indeed as Japan won a series of quick and impressive victories. The Japanese were exultant. After making little progress in a war with China, suddenly the Japanese controlled a wide area in

THE WAR IN THE PACIFIC

the South Pacific. Their visions of building a string of bases across the Pacific so strong that the United States and Australia would not dare attack them seemed possible.

After their successful attack on Pearl Harbor, the Japanese focused attention on the United States bases in the Philippines. The Philippines were a group of more than 7,000 islands that stretched over 1,100 miles across the western Pacific ocean. From the Philippines, the Japanese planned to take control of much of Southeast Asia and nearby Pacific islands. This area had rich supplies of oil, rubber and tin. These were extremely important materials for the Japanese military. The Japanese hoped that taking control of this area would also protect them from attack by the United States.

The Japanese believed that after they had taken over Southeast Asia and the Pacific the United States might be willing to negotiate. They believed that the United States would not want to fight in the Pacific Ocean after losing so many of its ships during the attack at Pearl Harbor. Japan mistakenly believed the United States would not be committed to fighting the war.[1]

The Philippines

Less than nine hours after the attack on Pearl Harbor, Japanese planes bombed Clark Field on the island of Luzon, in the Philippines. They demolished about one hundred of MacArthur's planes, all parked on the ground. The effectiveness of the United States Far Eastern Air Force was destroyed. The United States had controlled the Philippines since 1898, but now faced a Japanese invasion with few soldiers, ships, or planes.

Disaster followed disaster. On December 10, Japanese invaders landed on Luzon. Luzon is the biggest island in the Philippines and had the biggest city, Manila. American troops fought hard to save Manila. Faced with overwhelming numbers, Americans evacuated Manila and retreated to Bataan at the tip of the island. Finally, on April 9, 1942, after four months of fighting, the Americans surrendered. By June 9, all Philippine resistance to the Japanese had ended.

The Japanese were extremely cruel to their prisoners. After their surrender, American and Filipino prisoners were forced to march one hundred miles in what became notorious as the Bataan Death March. During the march 10,650 men died. In prison camp, 17,600 more died.

More Japanese Victories

Japanese forces swiftly conquered Hong Kong, and the islands of Borneo and Malaya. The Japanese also forced the Allies to retreat in Burma. The capture of the American islands of Guam on December 10 and Wake on December 22 gave Japan still more important bases.

The Japanese continued to have success after success during the early months of 1942. The Japanese military defeated the Allies, taking big cities like Hong Kong and Singapore as well as important islands like Guam, New Guinea, and Java. These victories helped Japan take control of Southeast Asia and the western Pacific.

The Doolittle Raid

On the morning of April 18, 1942, the startled crew of a Japanese fishing boat 720 miles east of Tokyo saw an American naval force steaming westward. The fishermen immediately radioed Yamamoto's headquarters. They had spotted Admiral William Halsey's task force, which included the carrier *Hornet*, transporting sixteen long-range B-25 Army bombers—far larger than normal carrier planes. The B-25s, under Lieutenant

On this anniversary of the attack upon Pearl Harbor let us—

REMEMBER AND HONOR
the men and women who have already given their lives in this struggle.

GIVE THANKS TO GOD
for our survival of the unprovoked attack by ruthless enemies.

TAKE STOCK OF
what we have done in one year of war and what lies ahead to be done in terms of Work-Fight-Sacrifice.

RE-DEDICATE
our strength, time, wealth and our very lives to preserve a concept of living more precious than individual life itself.

For our priceless Bill of Rights and our Constitution of the United States of America we will

WORK! FIGHT! SACRIFICE!

"REMEMBER PEARL HARBOR DAY"

DECEMBER 7, 1942

Remember Pearl Harbor became a rallying cry for the American war effort.

Colonel James Doolittle, were to take off within 500 *400 in more*
miles of the coast, bomb Tokyo, and fly on to China.

Halsey saw the fishing boat. Deciding not to put the carriers in peril by moving closer to the coast, Halsey ordered an immediate launching. An attack from that distance was not expected and the bombers met almost no opposition. They caused little damage, but the Japanese were humiliated: the sanctity of their homeland had been violated and it would not have happened had the fleet's carriers been at Pearl Harbor on December 7.

After all their initial successes, the Japanese were unsure how to proceed. Admiral Isoroku Yamamoto believed the capture of Midway, 1,136 miles west of Pearl Harbor, was a necessary preliminary to a Hawaii invasion. He thought he could lure the United States forces into battle there and defeat them, thus shortening the war—the only way he thought Japan could win.[2]

The Doolittle raid ended the opposition in Japan to an attack on Midway. It would surely bring out American naval forces in full, the Japanese believed, and they were confident they could win and be in a position to invade Hawaii. At any rate, they could add another island to their defensive chain.

On May 23 Imperial Headquarters ordered training to begin for the invasion of Hawaii. But first, of course, they had to seize Midway. That battle began on June 4.

Midway: The Japanese Are Halted

Admiral Yamamoto had hoped to destroy the United States Pacific Fleet at Midway. He instead suffered a stunning defeat. His complex plan called for part of his force to be sent to the western Aleutians, between Alaska and Japan, to confuse the Americans and to obtain defensive bases. He was not successful; American code-breakers learned about his plans.

The division of Japanese forces contributed to a United States victory at Midway. The aircraft carriers that had escaped the Pearl Harbor disaster were another factor. Japan lost four aircraft carriers, three hundred planes, hundreds of expert air crews and a heavy cruiser, while the United States lost one carrier and a destroyer. Yamamoto's force still had several carriers and a large surface fleet, but for the allies, the tide had begun to turn. General George Marshall, the Chief of Staff, said later: "The closest squeak and the greatest victory [in the Pacific] was at Midway."[3]

Midway ended Japanese plans to invade Hawaii. Australia, however, was another matter. That island continent was a rapidly increasing source of Allied manpower and military production, as American forces rapidly headed there. One good place from which to bomb Australia was Rabaul, which the Japanese had seized in January 1942. Another possible base for air strikes was Port Moresby, an Allied base in New Guinea, which the Japanese hoped to seize. After Midway, on the unoccupied island of Guadalcanal, the Japanese began to build a major air base.

An American soldier cautiously looks inside an evacuated Japanese bunker.

Retaking the South Pacific

Japan and the United States focused on New Guinea and the Solomon Islands, an island chain six hundred miles long. Both New Guinea and the Solomon Islands are between Hawaii and Australia. In the next year and a half thousands died over these islands in some of the most savage fighting of the war.

General Douglas MacArthur was now in command of the war in the Southwest Pacific. MacArthur wanted to return to the Philippines and then move on to Japan. On July 2, 1942, the United States began a two-pronged advance on New Guinea and the Solomon Islands. Admiral Chester Nimitz led an attack on the Japanese in the Solomon Islands. At the same time, MacArthur led a force that attacked the Japanese in the jungles of New Guinea.

The plan was initiated when a force of United States Marines landed on Guadalcanal, one of the Solomon Islands. Japanese soldiers building an air base on Guadalcanal were completely surprised. The epic struggle for the 2,250 square-mile island of Guadalcanal involved ships and planes as well as ground forces, and there were no easy times for anyone on land, sea, or air. Fear and fatigue were constant. In the jungle, disease was as big a challenge as the opposing troops. Mosquitoes bearing malaria seemed deadlier than the enemy.

Ground combat was probably the worst ordeal. A marine sergeant had this memory long afterward:

The real battle for Guadalcanal was in October [1942]. Both sides built up, and got in the middle of the ring. They wanted the airport and we wanted to hold it at all cost. That was it. They sent in ships, planes, everything. . . . It was the second night of the battle. There had been heavy action down the line. After all the noise earlier it was so quiet you could hear the men breathing. . . . I moved along the line warning the men not to fire yet but to let the Japs get close and then give them everything. . . . We heard soft muttering down in the jungle. . . . [S]omeone shrieked and all hell let loose. . . . It was a confusing struggle lit up by flashes from machine-gun fire. . . . In the flickering light I saw three Japanese charge. . . . I shot two of them, but the third ran through one of my gunners with a bayonet and actually lifted him into the air. I shot him too.[4]

In New Guinea, meanwhile, Japanese and American troops fought a "war of annihilation." Both sides also fought disease in jungles, swamps, and eight-foot tall kunai grass.[5] Every infantryman carried hand grenades. Each contained two ounces of TNT that could be thrown one hundred feet. They were used frequently on bunkers containing Japanese, who "had a habit of throwing our grenades back so we had to hold a four-second grenade for two or three seconds before hurling it."[6]

In September 1942 American air strikes and Australian ground troops forced the Japanese to halt their drive to Port Moresby, in New Guinea. On February 7, 1943, the last Japanese troops were forced to leave Guadalcanal, ending the long nightmare there.

Many difficult battles lay ahead in the Pacific, but the Japanese army had been forced to stop.

Closing In

Following the victory at Guadalcanal, Japanese and American troops fought over many more islands in the Pacific Ocean. The United States won victory after victory, but often at great cost. On the Island of Tarawa in the central Pacific, 4,500 Japanese and 1,300 Americans were killed. More than 2,000 more Americans were wounded in the battle. Step by step, American forces moved closer and closer to Japan. The United States wanted to get close to Japan to build airports for the new B-29 Superfortresses airplanes. Finally, Americans defeated the Japanese at the island of Saipan, on June 15 1944. Saipan was only 1,200 miles from Tokyo. The American victory at Saipan meant that B-29s could now easily drop bombs on Japan.

Another important step for the American military was to re-take the Philippines. Before leaving the Philippines in 1942, MacArthur vowed to return.

MacArthur finally got his chance to return. "They are waiting for me there—it has been a long time," said MacArthur.[7] In October 1944, the United States and Japanese navies faced each other in a epic sea battle at Leyte Gulf. Leyte was one of the Philippine islands, and the Japanese knew they must win to have any chance against the Americans. Using every weapon they could, the Japanese fought ferociously. A Japanese

American troops fighting against the Japanese in the South Pacific.

suicide weapon called "kamikaze" was introduced in Leyte Gulf. Planes were turned into human missiles as pilots crashed them into enemy ships. Even kamikazes were not enough to turn the tide. Despite high casualties, the Americans defeated the Japanese and destroyed four aircraft carriers, three battleships, and nineteen destroyers.

After the Leyte Gulf naval battle, in October 1944 United States troops landed on Leyte itself. Unexpectedly bitter fighting delayed a landing on the main Philippine island of Luzon until January. American troops reached Manila in February, but over 12,000 Americans died in the fighting, along with 16,000 Japanese soldiers and 100,000 Filipinos. The Philippines struggle finally ended on March 2, 1945. MacArthur had returned and conquered.

The Final Steps

Battle after battle, the American troops closed in on Japan. The island of Iwo Jima, 750 miles from central Japan, was next. The Japanese had built two airstrips on its volcanic soil and were beginning a third when the American troops landed early in February 1945. The attack was not unexpected and the Japanese fire that greeted it was vast and deadly, day and night. The fighting did not end until the end of March. Of the Marines who landed there, 6,821 were killed and 20,000 wounded. Nearly all the 21,000 Japanese defenders died in the fighting.

The Japanese were also prepared for an attack on the next island—Okinawa—400 miles closer to Japan. In the fighting from the April 1 landing until the resistance ended on June 21, up to 120,000 Japanese troops and 170,000 civilians died while 12,000 Americans were killed and over 33,000 were wounded.

Three days after the American victory at Iwo Jima, President Franklin Delano Roosevelt died on March 29, 1945. Roosevelt was the only president to be elected four times and had served as president through the Great Depression, Pearl Harbor, and most of World War II. Now the world's attention turned to his little-known vice president, Harry S. Truman. Would Roosevelt's death affect the American military? Roosevelt had guided America through difficult times and nobody knew whether Truman would display the same kind of leadership.

The problems confronting Truman would not be easy. In view of the high number of casualties at Iwo Jima, Americans worried about what would happen with an invasion of Japan. American military leaders had been instructed to plan an invasion. A landing on the mountainous island of Kyushu was scheduled for November 1945, and another on the main island of Honshu for March, 1946.

While the Japanese had been steadily forced to give ground, it was clear that they would keep on fighting, mainly because of the Allies' policy of demanding "unconditional surrender." This meant that the Allies—the United States, Britain, and the Soviet

THE WHITE HOUSE

WASHINGTON

I have to decide Japanese strategy — shall we invade Japan proper or shall we bomb and blockade? That is my hardest decision to date. But I'll make it when I have all the facts.

So you see we talk about more that "Cabbages + Kings and Sealing wax and things"

They talked of many things Shoes and sealing wax and cabbages and kings

President Harry S. Truman wrote in his diary about the many difficult decisions he had to make regarding the war.

Union—would dictate the terms of the surrender. There was no guarantee that the Japanese could keep their emperor, and so they fought all the harder.

Meanwhile, polls in the United States in the summer of 1945 showed that most Americans wanted revenge against Japanese Emperor Hirohito. Anger from the attack on Pearl Harbor had festered for four years. The anger was intensified by reports of extreme Japanese cruelty, some of which became public knowledge only after the war. Examples of these were biological experiments on humans and the dropping of "plague" bombs on Chinese cities to see if the Japanese could start outbreaks of disease. Also, during the war one million Koreans were brought to Japan to work as "virtual slaves."[8]

There were exceptions to the brutal treatment. One American woman held in a camp in the Philippines wrote of the relationship between Japanese guards and American prisoners, "They really liked each other."[9]

However, Japanese brutality was common. Some reports were false, but the true incidents were awful enough. They included "wounded Japanese using hidden hand grenades to kill their rescuers and themselves" and Americans captured on Guadalcanal whose livers were removed by a Japanese doctor without an anesthetic. The Japanese announced that as a matter of policy the crews of B-29 bombers who bailed out over Japan or who crashed at sea would be killed.[10]

The most Japanese prisoners held at one time by Americans was 5,424, of whom slightly over one percent died. The Japanese captured 95,000 Allied servicemen. More than one of every three American prisoners of war held by the Japanese—nearly 38 percent—perished, many of them horribly.

The Japanese were not alone in treating their enemy with contempt. The feeling that Japanese were subhuman was common among American servicemen. A general remembered, "Killing a Japanese was like killing a rattlesnake. I didn't always have that feeling in Europe about some poor German family man, but I felt with a Jap it was like killing a rattlesnake."[11]

Before sending troops to Japan, America started long-distance bombing raids. General Curtis LeMay decided to send B-29 bombers with no guns so they could carry even more bombs. On March 9, 1945, loaded with firebombs, B-29 bombers destroyed 16 square miles of Tokyo and left over a million homeless and 87,000 dead.

More bombing raids followed on Tokyo and other cities: 520 B-29s hit Tokyo on May 23 and 564 two days later; 450 hit Yokohama on the 29th; 599 hit Osaka and Nagoya on July 24. The attacks killed at least 241,000 and left 313,000 injured.

Despite the high casualties, Japan still did not surrender. The United States did have another option. For years, American scientists had been working to create an atomic bomb. This bomb would be much more powerful than any other bomb ever built. Finally, on July 16, 1945, they succeeded in testing the world's first atomic bomb. Deciding to use the bomb, however,

HQ U/S FOR_ES EUROPEAN _HEA_ER

STAFF MESSAGE CONTROL

INCOMING ~~TOP SECRET~~ MESSAGE

U R G E N T

FROM: AGWAR Washington

TO : Tripartite Conference Babelsberg, Germany

NO : WAR 41011   30 July 1945.

To the President from the Secretary of War.

The time schedule on Groves' project is progressing so rapidly that it is now essential that statement for release by you be available not later than Wednesday, 1 August. I have revised draft of statement, which I previously presented to you, in light of

(A) Your recent ultimatum;

(B) Dramatic results of test and

(C) Certain minor suggestions made by British of which Byrnes is aware,

While I am planning to start a copy by special courier tomorrow in the hope you can be reached, nevertheless in the event he does not reach you in time, I will appreciate having your authority to have White House release revised statement as soon as necessary.

Sorry circumstances seem to require this emergency action.

ACTION: Gen. Vaughan

VICTORY-IN-733   (31 July 1945)   3022173

~~TOP SECRET~~   COPY NO

THE MAKING OF AN EXACT COPY OF THIS MESSAGE IS FORBIDDEN

In this telegram from Secretary of State Stimson, President Truman is informed that the atomic bomb is almost ready for use.

Sec War

Reply to your 41011
suggestions approved
Release when ready
but not sooner than
August 2.

HST

President Harry S. Truman's reply to Secretary of State Stimson's telegram (on its back). Truman grants permission to use the bomb.

was not an easy decision. President Harry S. Truman described the atomic bomb in his diary as "the most terrible thing ever discovered."[12] Many people, including the well-known scientist, Albert Einstein, believed the bomb was too horrible to ever use. Still, Truman and many others hoped the bomb would help to end the war and save American lives that would be lost were the United States to invade Japan.

On August 6, at about 8:15 A.M. (Japanese time), a B-29 at 30,000 feet released the bomb, which exploded 1,900 feet above Hiroshima and destroyed most of the city. The exact number of deaths cannot be measured, but nearly 100,000 were killed instantly. Recent surveys give 130,000 as the total killed, including those who died from acute exposure to radiation.

On August 8 one and a half million Soviet troops invaded Manchuria and joined the war against Japan. A day later, a second atomic bomb was dropped on Nagasaki causing a death toll of between 60,000 and 70,000.

In Japan the emperor and his advisors, civilian and military, held two emotional conferences on the ninth and fourteenth of August. The militarist and peace factions remained divided, but it finally became clear to all that the only option to ending the war was suicidal resistance. On August 14 the Emperor signed a decree. It did not contain the word "surrender," but it ended the war.

Surrender and Occupation

In Tokyo Bay on the morning of September 2, 1945, aboard Nimitz's flagship, the battleship *Missouri*, an ordinary mess table covered with a green cloth was set up on the admiral's veranda deck. On the *Missouri* Japan's surrender was accepted by General MacArthur, the newly named supreme commander of the Allied Forces in Japan.

A few days after the signing, MacArthur established headquarters in the United States Embassy in Tokyo. An American flag that had flown in

The Japanese surrender, September 2, 1945.

Washington on the day of Pearl Harbor, and on *Missouri* during the surrender, was raised on the embassy flagpole. Japan was in chaos. Air raids had killed 670,000 of the 1,850,000 Japanese who had died in the war and many cities lay in ruins. There was very little food or clothing.

The Allied occupation was peaceful from the start, perhaps because people on both sides desperately wanted peace. One of them was Commander Mitsuo Fuchida, who had led the air attack on Pearl Harbor. Fuchida became a small farmer in his home town.

The news that the war was finally over caused jubilation all over America. One who did not celebrate was Signalman First Class Lee Ebner, who was on board the battleship *West Virginia* when the bombs fell at Pearl Harbor. Later he served on other ships in combat. When word came of the war's end, Ebner was on a ship in Subic Bay in the Philippines. He did not join other sailors as they jumped for joy. All he could think of was his friends who were not there, and the destruction he had seen. He "just sat down and rested his chin in his hands and stared at the deck."[13]

For Americans, World War II began at Pearl Harbor and ended at Nagasaki.

Many Americans remembered exactly where they were when they heard about the attack. Pearl Harbor became an important event that divided time. Before Pearl Harbor was the Great Depression, a time of high unemployment, poverty, and little hope. After Pearl Harbor was World War II. The war ended the Great Depression and brought Americans together to defeat Germany and Japan.

THE LEGACY OF PEARL HARBOR

By ending the Great Depression, Pearl Harbor did what America could not do alone. For twelve years Americans struggled during the Depression. Many, many Americans were unemployed, poor, and hungry during this period. After his first election, in 1932, President Franklin Delano Roosevelt enacted many programs to end the Depression—but it still continued.

Suddenly on December 8, 1941, America needed to rebuild its Navy and prepare for war against

Germany and Japan. For the first time since the Great Depression began, there were nearly enough jobs for everybody. Many American men enlisted in the army and navy. Some other men and many women found jobs helping the war effort. American workers built new airplanes and ships, and rebuilt the ships damaged at Pearl Harbor.

Pearl Harbor also changed American attitudes toward foreign wars. Before Pearl Harbor many Americans were isolationists. Famous people like aviator Charles Lindbergh and former President Herbert Hoover opposed the war. Many Americans heard of the horrible actions of Nazi Germany as they attacked Poland, France, and other countries, but they still did not want to fight the Germans. After bombs dropped on Hawaii, few people opposed involvement in World War II. America had been attacked and needed to defend itself. Before Pearl Harbor, entering the war seemed unthinkable. After Pearl Harbor, Americans joined the war-effort with gusto.

The bombing of Pearl Harbor also made many Americans suspicious of people of Japanese ancestry living in the United States. In the wake of Pearl Harbor, Japanese Americans and Japanese citizens living in the western United States faced violence and discrimination. In western states where many lived, all people of Japanese ancestry—even American citizens—came under suspicion. In February 1942, President Roosevelt ordered that "enemy aliens" be sent to internment camps. Japanese Americans lost

Dept #3

CONGRESS SHOULD COMPENSATE THOSE WRONGED.

THIS IS THE OPINION EXPRESSED BY JUDGE DENMAN OF THE
NINTH CIRCUIT COURT OF APPEALS IN HIS DISSENTING DECISION
ON THE KOREMITSU CASE ....DECEMBER 2nd.

He placed it in the following words...IT IS CUSTOMARY
FOR THE SUPREME COURT AND OTHER FEDERAL COURTS TO COMMENT,
WHERE CLAIMS OF OPPRESSION ARISING FROM CONGRESSIONAL LEGI-
SLATION ARE NOT REGUARDED AS MAKING THE LEGISLATION VALID
THAT THE CLAIMANT SHOULD LOOK TO CONGRESS FOR THIS REMEDY.

THIS MEANS...CONGRESS BY APPROPRIATE LEGISLATION SHOULD
AFFORD SOME COMPENSATION TO THE VICTIMS OF MILITARY ORDERS.

HE FURTHER STATES " IT IS WITHIN THAT PRACTICE TO STATE
THAT WHERE ,AS A WAR NECESSITY, SUCH WRONGS ARE DELIBERATELY
COMMITTED UPON IT'S CITIZENS BY A CIVILIZED NATION,ORDINARY
DECENT STANDARDS REQUIRE THAT COMPENSATION MUST BE MADE.

Lecture and discussion groups are now being arranged by
                KIYOSHI OKAMOTO
                CHAIRMAN...FAIR PLAY COMMITTEE
                22-8-B...Heart Mountain

If interested, please contact above chairman. Announcement will be made later.

最高裁判事デンマン氏は去る十二月
二日本権に対する松氏の事件に
付左の如く声明せる

未国議会は軍命の命令による豪
付擾害を文部に法律を制

定すべき場合

未国上校裁判所又は聯邦裁判所

訴権利を無として権利も正すべき法律も

也世未すべきである

比未国文明国に市民の自由と東縛

し不合理極まる未る可つ東律

民族を挙しのインデアンの境遇よ

十六条「法である

*Announcement of a meeting to protest the internment
of Japanese Americans, written in English and
Japanese.*

their jobs, their homes, and almost everything they owned and moved into cramped prison camps. Many Japanese and Japanese-Americans remained in these camps for years until nearly the end of the war.

Perhaps the most lasting impact of the bombing of Pearl Harbor is on the survivors and the families and friends of American soldiers who died that day. Since the attack, they have worked to keep the memory of Pearl Harbor alive and to honor those who died there. In 1960, the *U.S.S. Arizona* Memorial opened at Pearl Harbor floating above the wreckage of the *Arizona* battleship. The memorial serves as a reminder of the sacrifice of all the men and women who died in the attack and especially the thousand crew members who died on the *Arizona*.

★ TIMELINE ★

1931—*September 18*: Japan invades Manchuria, a region of China. Some historians consider the invasion of Manchuria to be the actual start of World War II.

1941—*September 22*: Japan invades French Indochina. In response the United States stops selling oil to Japan.
November 11: Japanese fleet leaves for Pearl Harbor.
November 27: United States War Department issues a "war warning" to all American military bases.
December 1: Japanese military officials make the final decision to attack Pearl Harbor.
December 7, 4:35 A.M. (Hawaii time): Japanese submarine spotted near Pearl Harbor.
December 7, 6:15 A.M.: First wave of Japanese airplanes takes off from Japanese carrier fleet.
December 7, 7:02 A.M.: Japanese airplanes spotted by American radar operators.
December 7, 7:03 A.M.: Japanese submarine sunk just outside the entrance to Pearl Harbor.
December 7, 7:56 A.M.: First wave of attack on Pearl Harbor begins.
December 22: Japan invades the Philippines.

1942—*February 19*: President Franklin D. Roosevelt signs Executive Order 9066, which allowed the military to relocate Japanese and Japanese Americans living in the United States.

April 18: James Doolittle leads American bombing raid on Tokyo.

June 4: United States defeats Japan in Battle of Midway.

1943—*February 8*: United States wins Battle of Guadalcanal.

1944—*October 21*: General MacArthur returns to the Philippines.

December: Relocation of Japanese and Japanese Americans ends.

1945—*April 12*: President Franklin Roosevelt dies. Harry S. Truman becomes president.

July 16: First atomic bomb test in New Mexico.

August 6: United States drops first atomic bomb on Hiroshima, Japan.

August 9: United States drops second atomic bomb on Nagasaki, Japan.

September 2: Japan surrenders to allies and ends World War II.

1988—*August 4*: The Civil Rights Bill of 1988 contains a formal apology to Japanese and Japanese Americans interned during World War II.

★ CHAPTER NOTES ★

Introduction

1. Gordon W. Prange in collaboration with Donald M. Goldstein and Katherine V. Dillon, *At Dawn We Slept: The Untold Story of Pearl Harbor* (New York: Viking Penguin, 1981), pp. 406–411.

2. Prange, *At Dawn We Slept*, p. 97.

Chapter 1. The Day Before

1. Gordon W. Prange with Donald M. Goldstein and Katherine V. Dillon, *December 7 1941: The Day the Japanese Attacked Pearl Harbor* (New York: McGraw Hill, 1988), pp. 41–42.

2. Gordon W. Prange in collaboration with Donald M. Goldstein and Katherine V. Dillon, *At Dawn We Slept: The Untold Story of Pearl Harbor* (New York: Viking Penguin, 1981), pp. 73–75.

3. Walter Lord, *Day of Infamy* (New York: Bantam, 1958), pp. 6–7.

4. Lord, *Day of Infamy*, pp. 7–9; Prange, *December 7*, pp. 35–41, 79.

Chapter 2. War or Peace?

1. John Toland, *The Rising Sun: the Decline and Fall of the Japanese Empire 1936–1945*, Vol. 1 (New York: Random House, 1970), p. 114.

2. David C. Evans and Mark R. Peattie, *Kaigun: Strategy, Tactics and Technology in the Imperial Japanese Navy 1887–1941* (Annapolis: Naval Institute Press, 1997), p. 606.

3. Gordon W. Prange in collaboration with Donald M. Goldstein and Katherine V. Dillon, *At Dawn We Slept: The Untold Story of Pearl Harbor* (New York: Viking Penguin, 1981), pp. 98–106.

4. Alvin D. Coox, "The Pearl Harbor Raid Revisited," *The Journal of American–East Asian Relations* (Fall 1994), p. 217; Prange, *At Dawn We Slept*, p. 445.

5. Walter Lord, *Day of Infamy* (New York: Bantam, 1958), p. 25.

6. Prange, *At Dawn We Slept*, p. 487.

Chapter 3. Early Warnings

1. Gordon W. Prange in collaboration with Donald M. Goldstein and Katherine V. Dillon, *At Dawn We Slept: The Untold Story of Pearl Harbor* (New York: Viking Penguin, 1981), pp. 495–496.

2. Gordon W. Prange with Donald M. Goldstein and Katherine V. Dillon, *December 7 1941: The Day the Japanese Attacked Pearl Harbor* (New York: McGraw Hill, 1988), p. 98.

3. Walter Lord, *Day of Infamy* (New York: Bantam, 1958), p. 48; Prange, *December 7*, p. 99.

4. Prange, *December 7*, pp. 109–110.

Chapter 4. The Attack

1. Gordon W. Prange with Donald M. Goldstein and Katherine V. Dillon, *December 7 1941: The Day the Japanese Attacked Pearl Harbor* (New York: McGraw Hill, 1988), p. 114.

2. Prange, *December 7*, p. 164; Rear Admiral Edwin T. Layton with Captain Roger Pineau and John Costello, *And I Was There: Pearl Harbor and Midway—Breaking the Secrets* (New York: W. Morrow, 1985), p. 312.

3. Gordon W. Prange in collaboration with Donald M. Goldstein and Katherine V. Dillon, *At Dawn We Slept: The Untold Story of Pearl Harbor* (New York: Viking Penguin, 1981), pp. 527, 553; Robert E. Sherwood, *Roosevelt and Hopkins: An Intimate History* (New York: Harper, 1948), p. 431; Frank Freidel, *Franklin D. Roosevelt: A Rendezvous With Destiny* (Boston: Little Brown, 1990), p. 404.

4. Prange, *December 7*, p. 120.

5. Robert La Forte and Ronald Marcello, eds., *Remembering Pearl Harbor: Eyewitness Accounts by U.S. Military Men and Women* (Wilmington: SR Books, 1991), p. 29.

6. La Forte, *Remembering Pearl Harbor*, p. 30.

7. Prange, *December 7*, pp. 142–144.

8. Michael Slackman, *Target: Pearl Harbor* (Honolulu: University of Hawaii Press, 1990), pp. 120–121.

9. Prange, *At Dawn We Slept*, p. 507.

10. Donald Goldstein, Katherine V. Dillon, and J. Michael Wenger, *The Way It Was: Pearl Harbor—the Original Photographs* (Washington: Brassey's, 1991), p. 98.

11. Slackman, *Target*, pp. 165, 167.

12. Slackman, *Target*, pp. 109–110; Prange, *December 7*, pp. 148–149, 153; Doris Kearns Goodwin, *No Ordinary Time* (New York: Simon and Schuster, 1994), pp. 328–330.

13. Walter Lord, *Day of Infamy* (New York: Bantam, 1958), pp. 93, 185–187.

14. Stephen B. Young, "God, Please Get Us Out of This," *American Heritage* (April 1966), p. 110.

15. Slackman, *Target*, p. 105.

16. Prange, *December 7*, p. 193.

17. Ibid., p. 295.

18. Slackman, *Target,* pp. 132–133.

19. Thomas B. Allen, "Pearl Harbor: A Return to the Day of Infamy," *National Geographic* (December 1991), p. 66.

20. Slackman, *Target*, pp. 146–150.

21. Kathleen Warnes, "Nurses Under Fire: Healing and Heroism in the South Pacific," in Gunter Bischoff and Robert L. Dupont, eds., *The Pacific War Revisited* (Baton Rouge: Louisiana State University Press, 1997), p. 140.

22. Warnes, "Nurses Under Fire," pp. 139–142.

23. Slackman, *Target*, pp. 148–152; Stanley Weintraub, *Long Day's Journey into War* (New York: Plume, 1992), pp. 247–248.

24. Lord, *Day of Infamy*, p. 127.

25. Prange, *December 7*, pp. 192–193.

Chapter 5. A Devastating Loss

1. Alvin Coox, "The Pearl Harbor Raid Revisited," *Journal of American–East Asian Relations* (Fall 1994), pp. 221–223; Samuel Eliot Morison, *The Rising Sun in the Pacific* (Boston: Houghton Mifflin, 1958), p. 127.

2. David Smurthwaite, *The Pacific War Atlas, 1941–1945* (New York: Facts on File, 1995), p. 27; Gordon W. Prange with Donald M. Goldstein and Katherine V. Dillon, *God's Samurai: Lead Pilot at Pearl Harbor* (Washington: Brassey's, 1990), pp. 38–41.

3. Coox, "Pearl Harbor Raid," p. 223; Rear Admiral Edwin T. Layton, with Captain Roger Pineau and John Costello, *And I Was There: Pearl Harbor and Midway—Breaking the Secrets* (New York: W. Morrow, 1985), p. 322.

4. Michael Slackman, *Target: Pearl Harbor* (Honolulu: University of Hawaii Press, 1990), pp. 263–271.

5. Ibid, pp. 236–237.

6. Coox, "Pearl Harbor Raid," p. 225.

Chapter 6. The Aftermath

1. Author interview with Martha Branneman Gibbs, October 9, 1997.

2. Michael Slackman, *Target: Pearl Harbor* (Honolulu: University of Hawaii Press, 1990), p. 205; Walter Lord, *Day of Infamy* (New York: Bantam, 1958), p. 168.

3. Doris Kearns Goodwin, *No Ordinary Time* (New York: Simon and Schuster, 1994), p. 295.

4. Mark Jonathan Harris, Franklin D. Mitchell, Steven J. Schechter, *The Homefront: America During World War II* (New York: Putnam, 1984), p. 29.

5. Harris, *Homefront*, p. 85.

6. Ibid., pp. 27–28.

7. Michael H. Hunt, *Crises in U.S. Foreign Policy* (New Haven: Yale University Press, 1996), pp. 110–111; Samuel I. Rosenman, *Working With Roosevelt* (New York: Harper, 1952), p. 311.

8. Warren F. Kimball, *Forged in War: Roosevelt, Churchill, and the Second World War* (New York: W. Morrow, 1997), pp. 122, 131; Goodwin, *No Ordinary Time*, p. 290; Harris, *Homefront*, p. 141.

9. Goodwin, *No Ordinary Time*, pp. 313–314.

10. Harris, *Homefront*, p. 39.

11. John W. Dower, *War Without Mercy: Race and Power in the Pacific War* (New York: Pantheon, 1986), p. 80.

12. Dower, *War*, pp. 79, 82; John Morton Blum, *V Was for Victory: Politics and American Culture During World War II* (New York: Harcourt Brace Jovanovich, 1976), pp. 155–167.

Chapter 7. The War in the Pacific

1. Wayne S. Cole, *Roosevelt & the Isolationists* (Lincoln: University of Nebraska Press, 1983), p. 508; H.P. Wilmott, *Empires in the Balance: Japanese and Allied Strategies to April 1942* (Annapolis: Naval Institute Press, 1982), pp. 141–142.

2. Mitsuo Fuchida and Masatake Okumiya, *Midway: The Battle that Doomed Japan* (Annapolis: Naval Institute Press, 1955), pp. 53–54.

3. Forrest C. Pogue, *George C. Marshall: Ordeal and Hope* (New York: Viking, 1966), p. 325.

4. Eric Bergerud, *Touched with Fire: The Land War in the South Pacific* (New York: Viking, 1996), pp. 311–312.

5. Bergerud, *Touched With Fire*, p. 38.

6. Ibid., pp. 299–302.

7. Ronald Spector, *Eagle Against the Sun: The American War with Japan* (New York: The Free Press, 1985), p. 294.

8. N. D. Kristof, "Japan Confronting Gruesome War Atrocity," *The New York Times*, March 17, 1995, p. 1; Mikiso Hane, *Peasants, Rebels, & Outcasts: The Underside of Modern Japan* (New York: Pantheon, 1982), p. 237.

9. Christopher Thorne, *The Issue of War: States, Societies and the Far Eastern Conflict of 1941–1945* (New York: Oxford University Press, 1985), p. 121.

10. Robert B. Edgerton, *Warriors of the Rising Sun: A History of the Japanese Military* (New York: Norton, 1997),

p. 283; John W. Dower, *War Without Mercy: Race and Power in the Pacific War* (New York: Pantheon, 1986), pp. 48–49.

11. James J. Weingartner, "Trophies of War: U.S. Troops and the Mutilation of Japanese War Dead, 1941–1945," *Pacific Historical Review* (February 1992), pp. 53–67.

12. J. Samuel Walker, *Prompt & Utter Destruction: Truman and the Use of Atomic Bombs Against Japan* (Chapel Hill: University of North Carolina Press, 1997), p. 1.

13. Roger Dingman, "Reflections on Pearl Harbor Anniversaries Past," *The Journal of American–East Asian Relations* (Fall 1994) p. 293; Arthur L. Kelly, *Battle Fire! Combat Stories from World War II* (Lexington: University of Kentucky Press, 1997), p. 14.

★ Further Reading ★

Bachrach, Deborah. *Pearl Harbor: Opposing Viewpoints*. San Diego: Greenhaven Press, 1989.

Black, Wallace, and Jean F. Blashfield. *Pearl Harbor!* Parsippany, N.J.: Silver Burdett Press, 1991.

Dunnahoo, Terry. *Pearl Harbor: America Enters the War*. New York: Franklin Watts, 1991.

Hopkinson, Deborah. *Pearl Harbor*. Parsippany, N.J.: Silver Burdett Press, 1991.

Lord, Walter. *Day of Infamy*. Fredericksburg, Tex.: Admiral Nimitz Foundation, 1991.

Nardo, Don. *World War II: The War in the Pacific*. San Diego: Lucent Books, 1991.

Rice, Earl. *The Attack on Pearl Harbor*. San Diego: Lucent Books, 1996.

Rice, Earl. *The Battle of Midway: Battles of World War II*. San Diego: Lucent Books, 1996.

Shapiro, William E. *Pearl Harbor*. New York: Franklin Watts, 1984.

Stein, R. Conrad. *The USS Arizona*. Danbury, Conn.: Children's Press, 1992.

Sullivan, George. *The Day Pearl Harbor was Bombed*. New York: Scholastic, 1991.

Wills, Charles. *Pearl Harbor*. Parsippany, N.J.: Silver Burdett Press, 1991.

★ Internet Addresses ★

USS Utah Historical Web Site
   <http://www.geocities.com/Pentagon/Barracks/3136/>

Photographic Look at the United States Navy During the Attack on Pearl Harbor
   <http://www.geocities.com/CapeCanaveral/Hangar/5115/Main.html>

Home page for the memorial to the USS Missouri at Pearl Harbor
   <http://www.ussmissouri.com/>

Web page dedicated to the USS Arizona
   <http://www.library.arizona.edu/images/USS_Arizona/USS_Arizona.shtml>

National Archives and Records Administration Online Exhibit of WWII posters
   <http://www.nara.gov/exhall/powers/powers.html>

★ INDEX ★